Introducing Liturgical Catechesis

Formation Sessions for the Parish

Nick Wagner

Resource Publications, Inc.
San Jose, California

Reprint Department
Resource Publications, Inc.
160 E. Virginia #290
San Jose, California 95112-5876
(408) 286-8505 voice
(408) 287-8748 fax

Library of Congress Cataloging-in-Publication Data
Wagner, Nick, 1957-
      Introducing liturgical catechesis: formation sessions for the parish / Nick Wagner.
            p.   cm.
Includes bibliographical references.
      ISBN 0-89390-566-6 (pbk. : alk. paper)
      1. Catechetics—Catholic Church. 2. Catholic Church—Liturgy. I. Title.
      BX1968 .W34 2002
      268' .82—dc21

                                                                                        2002004888

Printed in the United States of America.
02 03 04 05 06 | 5 4 3 2 1

Editorial director: Nick Wagner
Production: Romina Saha
Copyeditor: Tricia Joerger
Cover design: Nelson Estarija
Production assistants: Rebecca Ritger, Judy Clark

Contents

How to Use This Book

The sessions of this book were originally published as part of a newsletter, the purpose of which was to help parishes explore the possibilities and challenges of developing a more liturgically integrated catechesis in their communities. The ecclesial foundation for the newsletter and this book is the rites of the church and the *General Directory for Catechesis*.

My hope is that the information presented here will lead the reader to explore the teaching of the church on liturgy and catechesis with fresh eyes. Sometimes the grind of pastoral duty can deaden us to the thrilling and perhaps frightening challenge of the Gospel. The legislative language of church documents that attempts to codify that challenge can seem boring and a bit out of touch with real life. But I believe a careful reading of post-Vatican II church teaching—especially as it appears in documents such as the *Rite of Christian Initiation of Adults* and the GDC—sets us on a course for an exciting adventure. If some small but significant number of parishes followed both the spirit and the letter of post-Vatican II teaching, we would be a different church.

When considering how seriously and faithfully you believe your parish can adhere to some of the more difficult challenges, it may help to think more long term. Often times, goals that seem impossible to accomplish become easier to think and plan for if we imagine a three-year or five-year time line. If you had three years to accomplish an "impossible" task, what small step would you need to take this year to set you on the way?

Another way to make the tasks more manageable is to share the workload and responsibility. One of the distinctive features of liturgical catechesis is that it necessarily involves the entire community. So, while the content of the sessions is addressed to the head catechist of the parish (who often carries the title of Director of Religious Education), discussion questions have been added to the end of each session. The intent is that the DRE would gather with other members of the community to dream, brainstorm, and imagine how the catechetical processes in the parish can more effectively lead the community into a deeper relationship with Jesus.

Use this book to spark your imagination, your hopes, your possibilities. Use it with others to draw them into the conversation. And use it as a way to begin to dream about how your parish can become an exciting, vibrant community dedicated to bringing people into communion and intimacy with Jesus.

Intimate Communion with Jesus Christ

How does a parish catechize? That fundamental question shapes the spirituality of each faith community. The very *way* in which the question is answered catechizes because everything a parish does, even the way in which it asks and answers questions, catechizes. Parishes can choose to be more or less intentional or faithful about catechesis, but they cannot choose to *not* catechize.

Most parishes, realizing this to be the case, usually anoint someone with the imposing title: Director of Religious Education. The title changes from parish to parish, but the job descriptions look amazingly similar. First, teach our children the basics of the faith in such a way that they will not leave the church when they are 17. Second, with whatever time you have left, mount a successful adult education program, establish a year-round RCIA process (for adults, teens, and children), and assist the youth minister with the confirmation program.

Toward intimate communion with Jesus Christ

You may not want to hear that Pope John Paul II thinks that job description represents only part of what you are supposed to be doing. The aim of catechesis, according to the pontiff, is to bring everyone in the parish into "communion" and "intimacy" with Jesus Christ (*On Catechesis in Our Time* 5).

How in the world is that possible? How can you be responsible for the intimate faith life of every person in your parish? Well, it's not easy, but it is possible. This book aims to show you how to make that possibility a reality. It will not only show you *how* to do it but how to do it in such a way that you don't burn out from stress and overwork.

The key to success: team building

The key to bringing everyone in the parish into intimate communion with Jesus Christ is to understand and make full use of all the ministries of the parish. This means you have to become more of a collaborator, more of a consulter, more of a listener, and more of a team builder. You are probably already practicing these skills. Still, perhaps there is a way you can get better at them. Perhaps there is a way you can call others to share in your team-building efforts. This book will give you guides and suggestions to do that.

As the DRE in the parish, you need to see your ministry as the hub of all the catechetical efforts of the community. Every ministry catechizes; it is impossible for ministers *not* to catechize. So, as catechism-central, your concern needs to focus on *how* the other ministers are catechizing and *what* their catechesis is teaching about faith. In any parish, there are several, perhaps dozens, of ministers. But the areas of ministry tend to fall into four key areas, which may be headed by a person, by a committee, or by whoever happens to be available on a given day. Nevertheless, these four key areas are focal points of every parish's activities:

1. the **catechetical ministry**
2. the **liturgical ministry**

The pastoral ministry of the parish can oftentimes be divided into two components:

3. the **pastoral ministry within the parish**
4. the **pastoral ministry beyond the parish**

The *Rite of Christian Initiation of Adults* says those who want to become Christian are to be "given suitable pastoral formation and guidance, aimed at training them in the Christian life." We can assume that those who are already Christian will want to deepen their own formation as well. The rite lists four ways in which this is achieved (75):

1. by a suitable catechesis that acquaints them with the word of God and the dogmas of the church
2. by living and praying the liturgical life of the community
3. by following the example of the rest of the community as they live the Christian life
4. by working to spread the Gospel through the apostolic work of the community

You can see that these four signposts of catechesis—word, worship, community, and service—parallel the four key areas of ministry in a parish. In other words, if each area of ministry is done well, it catechizes. If you can work toward focusing each area of parish ministry on doing more of what it is already supposed to be doing, you will be catechizing the entire parish.

If you can, imagine for a moment that you don't have to prepare materials for 15 volunteer catechists next week and you don't have to prepare 300 first communion certificates and you don't have to meet with the liturgist to plan confirmation. What would you say is the most important thing about your job? It is difficult to guess the answer of each individual reader, but based on the work of most religious educators, it is not hard to assume that your answer has something to do with passing on faith.

If you can still imagine for a moment, imagine you could get every area of ministry in your parish to agree that the most important job of the *parish* is to pass on faith. That shouldn't be too hard to imagine.

Most pastors, most liturgists, most youth ministers, most school teachers also want to pass on faith. It is why they got into ministry in the first place.

Okay, one last leap of imagination. Imagine you could channel all that pass-on-the-faith energy into a single effort, a single direction, everybody working together. That may be harder to imagine, but it is doable. It may be difficult in your situation, but there are few places where it would be absolutely impossible. Perhaps your first response is to think, "Sure, it would be possible if we had a better pastor or a flexible liturgist or a competent youth minister." Resist that thought. As true as it may be, it won't help to think that way. Somehow, you need to turn the other ministers of the parish into your allies. Thinking of them as roadblocks only establishes them more firmly as roadblocks.

Think of them instead in the ideal way you would like them to assist in the catechetical effort of the parish. Think of their unique gifts and talents and how you can encourage those gifts to move the parish along in its work of passing on the faith. Think of the ideal way you can interact with each of these ministries to enable your community to come into intimate communion with Jesus Christ. Simply by asking yourself how that can be accomplished is a catechetical act. The very asking of the question moves your community into deeper communion with Jesus.

Focus: First things first

For example, a primary goal for the catechetical ministry of the parish is to give catechumens and the faithful an appropriate acquaintance with God's word. How would the primacy of God's word be strengthened if every catechetical session was related to the liturgical readings of the coming Sunday? How would your catechetical efforts be strengthened if every parish meeting began with a 15-minute reflection on the upcoming Sunday Gospel? How much catechesis would happen if bridal couples and baptismal preparation groups drew upon the planned readings to impart a theology of the sacrament to be celebrated?

A primary goal of the liturgical ministry is the full, conscious, and active participation of the assembly. How does catechesis happen by encouraging the liturgical planners to meet that goal? How does preparing children and adults to celebrate the liturgy well function as an act of catechesis?

Build a parishwide catechetical effort

A primary goal of the pastoral ministry of the parish is to teach parishioners how to use prayer as a support for their lives and as a strength for their apostolic efforts in the world. How does teaching the parish to pray more deeply enable catechesis? How does encouraging love of neighbor, both in the parish and in the world, also encourage catechesis?

Everything a parish does catechizes. Your colleagues in ministry may not think of what they do as catechesis, but they probably think of what they do as setting a good example. You can build on that to create a unified, parish-wide catechetical effort. Even your willingness to try, to die to yourself, to redouble your efforts in the face of initial resistance is a catechetical act. You teach by your example.

In the following sessions, we will focus on some of the specifics of how you can more effectively interact with your colleagues. Not all suggestions will work in every situation. However, you may get a new

idea or a fresh insight. One thing you cannot do is retire to your corner of turf and "do your own thing." That, too, catechizes, but it catechizes badly. Your job is not impossible, but it is important. This book can be a tool to help you discern what needs to be done and how to go about doing it. If you are successful, you will be able to accomplish the goal set out by the pope to bring everyone in the parish into communion and intimacy with Jesus Christ because all the ministries of the parish will be working toward the same end.

For discussion

☐ Identify the four key areas of your community's activities. How does each area catechize well? What are three things you can do better in each area?

☐ Where are most efforts at catechesis directed in your community? If you could wave a magic wand, what changes, if any, would you make?

☐ Who are the three or four people in your parish with whom you can brainstorm possibilities for the future? If you asked them to help you imagine how the ministries of the parish could be used to bring everyone in the community into intimate communion with Jesus, how would they respond?

Preventing Turf Wars

If you are like most religious educators, you probably wear many hats and have diverse responsibilities in your parish. Sometimes the diversity can be challenging and other times maddening. When the challenges begin to become a little too challenging, keep this thought in mind. You really only have *one* task:

> The definitive aim of catechesis is to put people not only in touch, but also in communion and intimacy, with Jesus Christ (*General Directory for Catechesis* 80).

Everything you do has as its goal putting people into intimate communion with Jesus. Think about what that means for a moment. It means that you may not have to worry as much that people know enough, attend enough sessions, fill out the proper forms, say the right words, do the right things, or follow all the instructions. All these things are important, but none of them is the goal. At the end of the day, if the catechetical ministry of the parish has put people in touch with Jesus, you have done your job.

So how do you do that? How do you put people in touch with Jesus every day? The first thing you have to do is get help. Catechesis cannot be a "Lone Ranger" ministry. You are going to need the help of the pastor, the liturgy planning team, the music ministry, the youth ministry, the parish school—all the ministries in the parish. The way to get all these helpers on board is to continually hold up the vision of catechesis in the parish. Tell them as often and in as many ways as possible that your goal is to put people in touch with Jesus—in communion and intimacy. Ask them, as often and in as many ways as you can think of, how they can imagine contributing to that goal.

Getting cooperation

The difficulty is that all of us are subject to turf-ism. All of us want to protect our corner of the parish and implement our programs in ways that we know are going to "work." We don't want a lot of bother and intrusion from people who really don't know what they are talking about. Unfortunately (or fortunately) the Gospel demands that we give up on that kind of thinking. To be in touch with Jesus means being in intimate communion with the others in our Christian community—even those we don't like very much. We don't necessarily have to become best friends with those we find difficult to be around, but we do have to find a way to work together to accomplish the primary goal.

There are two things to keep in mind when developing working relationships: boundaries and competency.

Boundaries

Sometimes turf wars develop because of a lack of clear boundaries. Some folks in ministry resist having clear boundaries because they see them as barriers. If that is true for you, try thinking of boundaries more like traffic lanes than like walls. By having clearly marked traffic lanes, everybody can get where he or she is going without crashing into one another. If you need to change lanes for some reason, you can. However, you need to signal your turn and wait until the coast is clear.

Good ministerial boundaries are best set up by having written job descriptions. This is true even of volunteer ministers. Let's imagine the youth minister and the liturgist engaged in a struggle over who plans the confirmation liturgy. If that task is set out in one or the other's job description, there could be little dispute about whose job it is. Another example might be a struggle between the DRE and the school principal about what first communion preparation program should be used by the children of the parish. A clear description of who is responsible for that decision could help avoid conflict. Or suppose the head communion minister took it upon herself to correct the way in which the teachers serve communion at a school Mass. Is that in her job description? If not, it would be easier to call her attention to the fact that she had crossed a boundary.

Good fences make for good neighbors and good boundaries can make for good ministry.

Competency

The next thing to be aware of is competency. Boundaries will not eliminate all turf wars because sometimes members of the team think a job outside their own area is not being done competently. The temptation is for the dissatisfied team member to attempt to take on the task so it will be done "right." Remember, though, the goal is not first of all to get things done right. The goal is to put people—even incompetent team members— in touch with Jesus.

And that is the key to understanding competency. Competency is not first of all about academic training. It is about the ability of the minister to put people in touch with Jesus. A music minister will do that through liturgical music, a liturgist through ritual prayer, a principal through teaching and administration, etc. Each of these ministers needs to be skilled and trained in his or her job in order to put people in touch with Jesus *through that ministry.* However, a musician can be a talented pianist but fail to bring people into intimate communion with Jesus. Competency for ministry is not just about how well a minister can perform the technical aspects of what is listed in the job description.

That does not mean, however, that proficiency at the required skills is unimportant. An interesting thing happens when a minister has a little—but not enough—training in his or her area. Undertrained ministers tend to be more defensive about what little they do know and tend to see "constructive criticism" as a threat to themselves. Well-trained ministers, on the other hand, are confident in their abilities

and can take criticism for what it is and not as a personal affront.

Let's suppose the DRE in the parish has done postgraduate study, has worked in parishes for 20 years, has served on the boards of several diocesan and national organizations, and has a working knowledge of all the catechetical documents relevant to parish ministry. In the same parish, the newly hired liturgist has served on the liturgy committee "forever," has been to the Los Angeles Liturgy Conference twice, has taken several of the liturgy courses in the diocesan lay ministry training program, and has a bachelor's degree in computer science. After a somewhat bumpy rite of acceptance into the order of catechumens, the DRE suggests at the next staff meeting that some time be set aside to evaluate the liturgy. Turf-ism begins to rear its head. It is not in the DRE's job description to evaluate the liturgy, and the liturgist, who must know things did not go well, feels threatened because he does not know *why* the liturgy did not go well.

Several things can happen in this example to avoid turf-ism, but the first is to take on a loving, gracious attitude. The DRE, in this example, is clearly the person who knows what should have been done and what did not work. The first question she needs to ask is: Did the rite put people in touch with Jesus? Liturgy, like most ministries of the church, is somewhat indestructible. No matter how badly we mess it up, the assembly still seems to find a way to pray. So, while the DRE may hope for better things next time, she can begin by acknowledging what worked. By staying within her own boundaries and focusing on the positive, the DRE can begin to build a trust relationship with the liturgist. It may take a year or more; however, that is the primary aim of catechesis— to put people in relationship with Jesus. Nothing is more important. Then, once a secure relationship is established, the DRE might be able to serve as a mentor to the new liturgist, guiding him to the proper coursework, commentaries, and concepts about liturgy.

Creative tension

It is important to point out the difference between turf wars and creative tension. In an ideal world, all ministers on the team are fully competent to do their ministries. That does not mean there will never be conflict. But the conflicts will be those that are bound to happen when everyone feels free to share his or her ideas, hopes, dreams, disappointments, and fears. Hopes and disappointments are not always going to mesh, and tempers may even flair a little. But if everyone believes in the overall vision and in the overall good will of those gathered, creative tension can lead to new insights and new ideas.

Dealing with discouragement

Avoiding turf wars completely is not possible. We are all fallible and subject to stress and frustration. However, if your primary goal is to put more and more people in touch with Jesus, you cannot afford to let turf-ism get in the way. You will have to struggle to find ways to overcome your own natural defensiveness and that of those you work with. By practicing these more open behaviors, you will likely get hurt. Someone else may not play by the same rules and may continue to make assumptions about you and refuse to cooperate with you. Every situation is different, but the general rule of thumb has to be go back and try again. When you think you cannot try any more, pray. What you cannot do, God can. The psalmist says:

> Though I am weak and poor,
> God cares for me.
> My help, my savior,
> my God, act now! (40:17 Liturgical Psalter).

My final suggestion is to pick your battles. Sometimes people can get into turf wars over insignificant issues. If you get stuck, ask yourself how important the issue is to you. Are you just defending your turf on "principle"? Even if it is an important issue, can you let go of it this time and hope for a better resolution next time? Will more people be touched by Jesus if you stand firm than if you turn the other cheek?

For discussion

- ❏ Gather your brainstorming group that we spoke of in the first session. Or gather the leaders of the ministries in your community. Together, list five things you do right now to help put people in touch with Jesus. List five things you wish you did or wish you did better.
- ❏ What are the turf issues in your parish that prevent effective catechesis? Are there one or two things you can change about *yourself* that will help to lower the tension levels?
- ❏ What are your three most important goals for making catechesis more effective in your parish? What three issues can you let go of?

Using Liturgical Catechesis

Something has gone terribly amiss in the way we understand catechesis and the way it takes place in our parishes. This is how it was in the beginning: "They devoted themselves to the apostles' teaching and fellowship, to the breaking of bread and the prayers" (Acts 2:42). That was it. That was enough. It was from this simple process that the early Christians learned about and deepened their faith.

As a religious educator, your job is to facilitate the catechesis of everyone in the parish. The sole aim of catechesis is to draw people into intimate communion with Jesus (see Session 1). In order to enable everyone in the parish to enter into intimate communion with Jesus, you are going to have to call upon the skills of the other ministers in the parish (see Session 2).

The place where all the ministries of the parish converge and the place that best models the catechetical process used by the New Testament community is the liturgy. What has gone amiss is that most catechetical processes are not centered on the liturgy. In fact, any process identified as "liturgical catechesis" is sometimes seen as *inferior* to other types of religious education and, amazingly, is even "banned" in some places.

Is liturgical catechesis right for your parish?

This is really a false question. Liturgical catechesis happens. The question should be: Is liturgical catechesis done well or poorly in your parish? The liturgy will always catechize. If you teach children in a classroom setting that God loves them, but their liturgical experience is one of boredom or even hostility, they will usually not grow up "learning"

that God loves them. On the other hand, if children experience vibrant, exciting liturgies that put them in intimate communion with Jesus, but their religious education process is boring or unsound, they will still come to know that God loves them. The liturgy is the strongest catechetical tool you have in the parish. Your challenge as a religious educator is to learn how to take full advantage of it so that the children, the teenagers, the adults and the newcomers will all have both vibrant liturgical experiences and vibrant catechetical experiences.

And it's not that hard. It takes some vision and some skill, but creating a powerful catechetical process based on the liturgy can be easier than creating a classroom- style religious education program. The hardest part, for both you and your catechists, is to learn to let go of pre-planned agendas and outcomes. Some people cannot get past that first hurdle. But for those who can, an exciting adventure in faith-building awaits.

Key elements

The first step in creating a liturgical catechesis process is to get the right textbook. The right textbook for this process is the liturgy (which includes Sunday Mass, seasonal celebrations, and sacramental celebrations). This is so because the church "in the course of the year ... unfolds the whole mystery of Christ from his Incarnation and Nativity through his Ascension, to Pentecost and the expectation of the blessed hope of the coming of the Lord" (*Constitution on the Sacred Liturgy* 102 § 2). In the liturgy, the whole mystery of Christ—everything we are to believe—is revealed to us. Just as the New Testament community did, we devote ourselves to the teaching of the apostles (the word of God), fellowship

11

(celebrating with the members of our parish), breaking the bread (Eucharist), and the prayers (the Lord's Prayer and the other intercessory prayers of the liturgy).

The next step is to understand the ways in which catechesis can enhance the experience of the liturgy so that the whole mystery of Christ can be more effectively revealed. Catechesis can first of all prepare the faithful to celebrate the liturgy. By helping the assembly— especially newer members—learn the prayers and gestures of the liturgy and learn some of the basic meanings of the rituals and symbols, you will be helping the members of your community enter more fully into the liturgical celebration.

The second way in which catechesis interacts with the liturgy is mystagogically. Mystagogical catechesis is a catechesis that "reveals the mysteries." It is catechesis that usually happens after a liturgical celebration, and it is a reflection on the liturgical experience. In mystagogical catechesis, the catechist focuses on helping us go back over the experience in our minds and come to some insight about what it is we just celebrated. That catechist helps us make more concrete the experience of the mystery of Christ we had entered into in the liturgy. Mystagogical catechesis is both challenging and exciting. The challenge is to prepare for the catechetical session in a way that leaves the outcome open to the Spirit. It is not possible to pre-plan what the Spirit will reveal. The excitement arises from the fact that new aspects of Christ's mystery will be revealed not only to the participants but to the catechist as well.

The *Rite of Christian Initiation of Adults* identifies four aspects of a well-developed liturgical catechesis that can be summarized as word, worship, community and service (75). A catechized person is exposed to God's word on a regular basis. Note, however, that this is neither a random nor strictly sequential biblical study. It is a "hearing" of the word in a way that is accommodated to the liturgical year—that is, it is a *liturgical* word.

A full catechesis also involves full, conscious and active participation in the liturgical life of the church. This means celebrating Mass and participating in the sacramental life of the church and even in the celebration of the Hours.

One of the more essential things a catechetical program needs to promote is that we are a community,

an interdependent body. A well-catechized person will be conscious of the need to contribute to the welfare and building up of the body. Our model and source of inspiration for building up the body comes from the liturgy, where we become one with the Body of Christ.

And finally, a sound catechetical process will promote the advancement of God's reign through evangelization, apostolic works, and service to the whole world. This is ultimately the core of our mission as Catholics, and it is the charge left to us by Jesus— to go forth and proclaim the good news. This is also a liturgical charge. The reason we celebrate liturgy is to learn and rehearse how we are to live in the world. The liturgy ends with the mandate to go in peace to love and serve the Lord.

What about the Catholic stuff?

The critics of liturgical catechesis seem to fear that if we center our catechesis on the liturgy we will be leaving out a lot of essential information. They want to know when we teach the Catholic stuff. When do we teach the doctrine? It is difficult to pin down exactly what they think will be left out, but a partial list might include some of the following: Marian beliefs and practices, the teachings on abortion and birth control, the difference between Protestants and Catholics, the Pope, stations of the cross, confession, transubstantiation, salvation history, and Scripture.

Let's imagine for a moment that a Catholic child participates in a structured liturgical catechesis process for six years. That means the child would celebrate the three-year lectionary cycle twice. In that time, the child would be exposed to several Marian feast days on which Marian devotional practices such as the rosary could be explored. A child might be too young to become very involved in abortion and birth control issues, but many of the Gospel readings could lead to a discussion of the church's consistent life ethic. Easter season, with its focus on Acts and the tensions involved in forming the church, could lead to an exploration of the Protestant split and an explanation of church hierarchy and the role of the Pope. Stations and sin and reconciliation can be dealt with in Lent every year. Eucharist as meal and sacrifice can be discussed any Sunday. Salvation history is revealed over time as the riches of Scripture are proclaimed in the assembly every week. And the importance of Scripture itself in the life of the church is made clear by its central role in the liturgy.

One of the advantages of liturgical catechesis is that it is "spiral" rather than "linear." That means someone is not exposed to a doctrine or practice only once at a particular "grade level." Rather, the teachings and practices of the church are interwoven in a repeating cycle throughout each liturgical year. If a participant misses a session or even an entire year, he or she will still encounter all the basic beliefs of the church.

A "spiral" form of catechesis is also an advantage for developing an adult religious education process in your parish. Since liturgical catechesis is not linear, it does not have a beginning or ending point. There is no "graduation" from liturgical catechesis. Liturgical catechesis can be seamless and lifelong. The mystery of Christ is continually unfolded as participants celebrate the liturgical cycle over and over throughout their lives.

None of this happens automatically, of course. It requires a careful, spirit-filled catechetical team that is willing to put in the preparation and prayer required to lead people deeper into the paschal mystery. But the liturgy provides everything you need to be able to get started. It is an excellent textbook for "teaching" people how they can find intimate communion with Jesus.

For discussion

- ❑ Gather your brainstorming team that we discussed in Session 1. Discuss how your liturgical celebrations catechize. What three things can you suggest to make your celebrations more effective as catechetical "textbooks"?

- ❑ How can you create more mystagogical moments within your community? For example, can you provide family discussion questions based on the liturgy that can be sent home every week? What other ideas can you imagine?

- ❑ How would you explain to your catechists the differences between "spiral" and linear" catechesis? Are your catechetical efforts more linear or more spiral?

Adapting Catechesis:
A Look at the
General Directory for Catechesis

It is—or it should be—the goal of every religious educator to "put people not only in touch but in communion, in intimacy, with Jesus Christ" (*On Catechesis in Our Time* 5). The *General Directory for Catechesis* (1992; a revision of the 1971 *General Catechetical Directory*) expands on that central premise and seeks to help parishes catechize by making this important point:

> Catechesis has to be "contextualized" or adapted so that it adequately meets the needs of those it seeks to serve.

This is crucial for an effective catechetical process. Putting people in touch with Jesus is not only the goal of the religious educator but of every Christian. Helping others know Jesus is the heart of the Christian mission. The *General Directory for Catechesis* says there are three "essential moments" of evangelization (49):

1. missionary activity directed toward nonbelievers,
2. initial catechesis for seekers and catechumens, and
3. pastoral activity directed toward the Christian faithful.

In order for a catechetical process to be effective, religious educators need to understand that this three-fold evangelization process takes place in a diverse and changing world—even if that world is as small as your parish neighborhood. It is increasingly likely that within your parish boundaries there are people who have never heard the Gospel, people

who are fervent believers, and people who are baptized but separated from the church. Your catechetical efforts have to be adapted to fit the needs of each of these groups.

The *General Directory for Catechesis* tells us that the catechetical activity directed at these three different groups is not supposed to be three separate programs. The efforts overlap, merge, and enrich one another. The primary task of the church, however, has always been outreach to those who have never heard the Gospel. Our catechetical efforts have to be designed around this paradigm. To that end, the *General Directory for Catechesis* says that the model for *all* catechesis—even to the fervently faithful—is the baptismal catechumenate. "This catechumenal formation should inspire the other forms of catechesis in both their objectives and in their dynamism" (59). And, the document stresses, adult catechesis is to be considered the chief form of catechesis.

In short, our catechetical processes should be oriented primarily to adults who have never heard God's word, and the rest of our efforts—toward the faithful and the fallen-away Christians—should be modeled on and inspired by the catechumenate.

This is both frightening and freeing. It is frightening because most of us do not have programs like this. The *General Directory for Catechesis* calls us to do something radically new. (New for most of us, but ancient in the history of the church.) It is freeing because in our heart of hearts it is what most of us want to be doing. We want to tell the Good News to people who have never heard it and experience anew with them the complete joy we experienced when we first came to faith.

Tossing the baby with the bath water?

But what about all our programs? What about our baptismal preparation program for new parents? What about getting the children ready for first communion? What about getting all the "basics" taught before they become teenagers, get confirmed and leave the church? What about our Engaged Encounter retreats? What about the RENEW process we just started or the new Bible-study group that had a record 15 people show up last week? Are we supposed to abandon all that?

Obviously we cannot quit cold turkey on all our current structures. Maybe there are some we shouldn't quit on at all. But the real secret to doing effective catechesis is to direct all those current programs toward an outreach to all the potential catechumens in our neighborhoods. "In this way catechesis, situated in the context of the church's mission of evangelization and seen as an essential moment of that mission, receives from evangelization a missionary dynamic which deeply enriches it and defines its own identity (59)."

In other words, if parishioners believe they have a real stake in "an essential moment" of the church's mission, if they believe what they do makes a difference, catechesis will naturally become dynamic. People will seek it out so they will be able to make a more effective contribution to the mission. Wasn't that what happened to you? Didn't you one day wake up and realize you could make a difference? And didn't you then go seek out the training you needed to do the job you thought needed to be done? If we can convince some of our parishioners there is a job to be done—through whatever structures we now have in place—their enthusiasm will spread. They will tell fellow parishioners. They will tell their fallen away friends and family. If you've worked with catechumenate teams, you've seen this happen. The *General Directory for Catechesis* is asking that we move our evangelization efforts beyond just the small group that runs the catechumenate and make it the

primary effort of the entire parish. If we can do that, we will have no problem creating effective catechetical programs.

Given that outreach to unbelievers is the model for all parish activity, the catechumenate becomes the model for all catechetical activity.

Inspiration for adaptation

The *General Directory for Catechesis* notes, however, that there is an essential difference "between the *pre-baptismal* catechesis and the *post-baptismal* catechesis" received by newcomers to the faith. Post-baptismal catechesis flows from the sacramental celebrations of the church. With that distinction in mind, the *General Directory for Catechesis* lists several elements of the catechumenate that ought to be considered as inspirations for all catechetical activity.

- The catechumenate serves as a constant reminder to the whole parish of the vital importance of initiating new people into the community. The essential components of initiation are catechesis and the celebration of the initiation sacraments—baptism, confirmation, and Eucharist.
- The catechumenate is the responsibility of every member of the parish. This is a radical decentralization of the missionary activity of the church and requires every Christian to think of himself or herself as an equal partner in the work Jesus left us.
- The catechumenate is steeped in the mystery of Christ's death and resurrection. Therefore everyone involved in the work of initiation must work hard to clearly reveal the paschal nature of our faith. The Easter Vigil is the source and inspiration for all catechesis.
- The catechumenate is also an initial starting point for inculturation. The Son of God became human in a concrete place and time in history. That is to say, Jesus had a culture. Therefore, we accept and celebrate the cultures of all those who seek to become members of our church. Different cultures hear the word of God in different ways, and it is our job to find ways

of incorporating all those different styles of hearing into the catholicity of the church.

- Finally, we understand the catechumenate to be "*a process of formation*" (91). The catechumenate is not a textbook to be gotten through nor a series of meetings to attend nor a required number of service projects. It is a comprehensive formation, gradually accomplished in definite stages. It is marked and celebrated in "meaningful rites, symbols, biblical and liturgical signs" (91). Most of all, it is a formation handed on by us, the Christian faithful, the Body of Christ.

It is these principle elements of the catechumenate that the *General Directory for Catechesis* says should inspire the catechesis we provide for the faithful and the fallen-away Christians. You can use these central elements of the catechumenate as a kind of checklist for your parish. Do your catechetical efforts focus the parish toward initiation as the central mission of the parish? Do your catechetical efforts empower your parishioners to take up their cross of responsibility for the success of the parish mission to unbelievers? Do your catechetical efforts focus passionately on revealing the paschal mystery that we celebrate in its fullness in the Easter Vigil every year? Do your catechetical efforts instill in your parishioners a respect for and a joy over the various cultures in your community and neighboring communities? Finally, do your catechetical efforts make up a comprehensive, gradual formation process that takes place in well-marked stages, celebrated in the signs and symbols of the liturgy?

When designing your other catechetical efforts, you are not supposed to slavishly imitate the catechumenate, and you always have to remember you are dealing with baptized people. However, the central elements of the catechumenate—as outlined in the *General Directory for Catechesis*—can enrich your efforts to adapt how you do catechesis in your parish.

For discussion

- ❑ Of the GDC's three essential moments of evangelization, where is your parish strongest? Where does your parish need improvement?
- ❑ What are the central elements of the catechechumate that can be applied to your parish catechetical efforts?
- ❑ What are some strategies you can use to convert your current parish programs into catechetical processes modeled on the catechumenate? What suggestions does your brainstorming team have to offer?

A Useful Catechetical Tool: Introduction to the Revised *Lectionary for Mass*

The second edition of the *Lectionary for Mass* provides a powerful catechetical tool available for your community. The undiscovered gem is the Introduction. The Introduction to the second edition has been considerably expanded. "It provides an extended theological introduction to the proclamation of the word of God in the life of the Church and the liturgy," according to Father James Moroney, executive director of the bishops' secretariat for the liturgy.

As the chief catechist for your community, you will want to familiarize yourself with this new resource. The Introduction can, for example, help you explain the significance of the word of God in the liturgy. The text points out that the many riches of the word are "brought out in the different kinds of liturgical celebration and in the different gatherings of the faithful who take part in those celebrations." The way this happens, of course, is through the unfolding of the mystery of Christ throughout the liturgical year. But it also takes place "as the faithful respond individually to the Holy Spirit working within them. For them the liturgical celebration ... becomes a new event and enriches the word itself with new meaning and power" (3).

I don't know about you, but I'd want to call up every parishioner I know and tell them that we need them to be at Mass next Sunday because *their* individual response "enriches the word itself with new meaning and power." That is a message that has not gotten through to the faithful. If you rephrase the sentence in the negative, you get a sense for the importance of the participation of the faithful. If the faithful *do not* respond, the liturgy *does not* become a new event and the word *is not* enriched with new meaning and *is not* enriched with power.

How do the faithful respond in such a way that the word is enriched with new meaning and power? The first response is one "of listening and adoring 'in Spirit and in truth' (Jn 4:23)" (6).

Listening might seem like a passive response and might seem to go against the grain of the Second Vatican Council's call for full, conscious and active participation in the liturgy. But to truly listen is to hear the word deep within in our hearts. We listen with such an intensity that the word changes us. When I was a child, my mother would sometimes yell out, "Why don't you ever listen to me?" I certainly couldn't keep from "hearing" her. But I wasn't taking what she said to heart. I was not changing my behavior so it would reflect the spirit and truth of the word she had spoken to me. So it is with God's word and our required response:

> The Holy Spirit makes that response effective so that what is heard in the celebration of the liturgy may be carried out in a way of life: "Be doers of the word and not hearers only" (Jas 1:22). The liturgical celebration and the participation of the faithful receive outward expression in actions, gesture, and words .... Accordingly, the participation of the faithful increases to the degree that, as they listen to the word of God proclaimed in the liturgy, they strive harder to commit themselves to the Word of God

incarnate in Christ. Thus, they endeavor to conform their way of life to what they celebrate in the liturgy, and then in turn to bring to the celebration of the liturgy all that they do in life (6).

When our parishioners look at the face of God, do they see a frustrated mother yelling out, "Why don't you ever listen to me?" Or do they see a divine face of contentment and joy because we have become *doers* and not just *hearers*? Have we listened in spirit and truth? How do we know for sure? How does the world know?

> In the hearing of God's word the church is built up and grows, and in the signs of the liturgical celebration, God's wonderful, past works in the history of salvation are presented anew as mysterious realities. God in turn makes use of the congregation of the faithful that celebrates the liturgy in order that his word may speed on and be glorified and that his name be exalted among the nations (7).

I'm a news junkie, and I haven't heard any reports lately of God's name being exalted among the nations. I wouldn't be surprised if the face of God looked a little frustrated right now. We obviously have more to do to help our parishioners listen more actively to the word of God in the liturgy.

The Introduction goes on to describe some of the necessary elements required to make the Liturgy of the Word effective. These include the three readings from the Scripture and the psalm. The order of these readings "is an arrangement … that provides the faithful with the whole of God's word." The choice of readings was determined in order to give the faithful a greater understanding of our Christian faith and of the history of salvation (60). The order and choice of the readings is, itself, a catechetical tool: "The celebration of the liturgy is not in itself simply a form of catechesis, but it does contain an element of teaching." The lectionary, therefore, "deserves to be regarded as a pedagogical resource aiding catechesis" (61).

The Introduction also explains the various ministries involved in the Liturgy of the Word, including the ministry of the faithful. "As a help toward celebrating the memorial of the Lord with eager devotion, the faithful should be keenly aware of the one presence of Christ in both the word of the God … and 'above all under the eucharistic species' (Second Vatican Council, *Constitution on the Sacred Liturgy, Sacrosanctum Concilium,* n. 7)" (46).

In addition, when the faithful "hear the word of God and reflect deeply on it, [they] are enabled to respond to it actively with full faith, hope, and charity through prayer and self-giving, and not only during Mass but in their entire Christian life" (48).

By being aware, by truly hearing the word of God and reflecting on it deeply, the faithful are carrying out our active ministry within the Liturgy of the Word. Our participation in the liturgy enables us to grow more deeply in faith and enables us to become more self-giving.

How are the faithful, then, supposed to go about growing in awareness and reflecting deeply on the word? That's where you come in. First of all, you will want to work with your liturgical planning team to be sure the Liturgy of the Word is celebrated in such a way that it facilitates awareness and reflection. That at least means the readings must be proclaimed with passion and sincerity. You can also assist the faithful by providing opportunities for reflection before and after the liturgy. You might design a simple, short faith-sharing process based on the Sunday readings that could precede all parish meetings. You might list two or three discussion questions along with the citations of the readings in the Sunday bulletin. Get together with your catechists and brainstorm at least 10 other ideas.

It is the job of the faithful to celebrate the liturgy in such a way that we are changed. Our changed selves can then go out and change the world. If we do that well, if we do it often enough, and if enough of us do it, I will probably someday hear a national news report that begins: "Our top story tonight: God's name exalted among the nations. World leaders stunned as mass demonstrations gather to glorify God's word. Details at 11:00."

Well, maybe not. But *your* job is to catechize the parish so they know that's the goal. Somebody has to set out the target and challenge the parish to aim for it. The chief catechist of the parish is charged with bringing the faithful more deeply in touch with God's word.

Fortunately for you, the *Lectionary for Mass: Introduction* is an excellent tool to help you with that task.

For discussion

❐ Gather your brainstorming team and read through the Introduction to the Lectionary for Mass together. Write down ideas, images, thoughts, and questions that come to you.

❐ How strong is the individual response of your parishioners to the proclamation of the word? How can their response be strengthened? How can the work of the liturgy team, lectors, homilists, cantors, and catechists help make the Liturgy of the Word more effective?

❐ How can you better use the lectionary as a "pedagogical resource"?

Fasten Your Seatbelts: Things May Get Bumpy

The new *General Directory of Catechesis* says that all catechesis should be based on the baptismal catechumenate (59). Once you read that, you may imagine the "fasten seatbelt" sign flashing, the oxygen masks dropping from the roof of the cabin, and smoke pouring from the left engine. The prospect of breaking out of our current classroom-model mold and trying to move toward a catechumenal style is so frightening that early reactions identified that part of the GDC as a weakness to be concerned about.

On the contrary, the call for baptismal-style catechesis is one of the major strengths of the document. Here's why: Learning about faith is different than learning about religion.

However, the two are not completely exclusive; religious education involves faith building, and those who are seeking to grow in faith will need to learn some facts about what the church teaches. But the emphasis and the style with which religion and faith are communicated are very different.

Some people are fond of saying faith is caught, not taught. What they mean by this is that faith is "taught" in the same way we are taught to play. We are first "evangelized" to play. We see someone playing, and we like what we see. Then we are "converted." We become convinced that we too want to be players. Once we are converted, we mimic the things we see. Those who are better at playing than we are give us feedback. "Good shot." "Nice swing." "Yes! That's it!" We "learn" from our mistakes and from the praising we get when we do well. We ask for help. "How do you get it to spin like that?" Pretty soon we've mastered enough basic techniques that we can "teach" someone else how to play.

We join a team, we get a coach, we practice. These are the ways we learn to play. Much later, after we have become pretty good players, we might take a class on the fundamentals of the game or about the history of the sport. But most of us never do that. Most of us learned to play from those we saw playing, and we continue to learn by playing with those who are better than we are. We also learn by teaching other newcomers to play.

Faith happens the same way. That is what is so important about the insight of the GDC. The document recognizes that newcomers are not going to go to school to learn about faith. They are not going to come to a class; they are not going to read a book; they are not going to come to an after-Mass "Know Your Faith" session. The *only* way people come to faith is when they see other people living their faith. Okay, maybe one or two people come to faith when the airplane starts going down, but mostly it happens because of the way you and I buy groceries, greet people on the street, raise our kids, or vote. People come to faith because faithful people live faithfully. People come to faith because of our example.

The way to *teach* people about the faith is to be better examples. Exemplary faith, according to the RCIA, is evidenced in four different ways: through word, through worship, through community, and through service. According to the catechumenal model, newcomers to the faith are apprenticed into these four elements of our tradition through the following process.

- Catechesis is accommodated to their level of understanding. That means no canned programs. It means lots and lots of active listening. It means not expecting the candidates to answer our questions before we have answered theirs.

- Catechesis flows from and to the liturgy. Our faith is most fully expressed in the celebration of the paschal mystery in the liturgy. Good liturgy is the most effective form of catechesis we have.
- Catechesis happens in small groups. Good catechesis is not going to happen in groups of 100 or even 50. Groups need to be small enough that no one feels anonymous or unaccounted for. Faith gets built when everyone feels like they are on the team.
- Catechesis happens in stages. These stages *cannot* be predetermined or scheduled. The candidate moves to a new stage when the Spirit directs, not when we do.

So what does all this mean for your catechetical effort?

It means first of all that the primary catechetical effort of the parish is directed toward *adults who have not heard the Gospel.* ("Please make sure your tray tables and seat backs are in their full, upright and locked position.")

It means that the bulk of your secondary effort will be directed toward the faithful adults of the parish, most of whom are parents and grandparents. It means very little of your time will be spent teaching religion to children.

It will never happen, you're thinking. Great idea, but just not possible. We're stretched to the bone right now. How are we possibly going to reach out to adults, and unchurched ones at that?

Parishes have been saying the same thing ever since the predecessor to the GDC—the *General Catechetical Directory*—came out almost 30 years ago. Now the new GDC reiterates, in even stronger language, the call for our catechetical efforts to focus on adults. Either the people who write these things are completely out of touch, or there is some other way we are supposed to be doing things. For the sake of argument, let's assume church leaders are *not* out of touch. ("If you are assisting a child, place the mask over your own face first, then over the child's.")

If we assume our leaders know what they are talking about, does that mean you have to immediately

dismantle your current structure—the one you spent so many years building up, begging volunteers to help with, and battling for adequate funding? No it doesn't. You have, no doubt, created many good things. Your challenge is to take all the good things and build on them. If your current program has a solid foundation, it should be relatively painless to help it evolve into a process based on the GDC.

Here is a not-quite-monumental step to try. Next time you are getting ready to prepare children for first communion, select a sample group of parents with whom to try something new. The "sample" can be as large or small as your stress level can manage. Consider them a pilot group.

With this pilot group, your goal is to incorporate as many of the principles of the baptismal catechumenate as possible. Your goal with this group is to focus on the parents as the primary catechists of their children. You are not so much interested in catechizing the children as you are their parents. You want to catechize the parents in such a way that they are able to prepare their own children for first communion. So instead of having 12 sessions with the children and maybe two parent meetings, you would have 12 (or however many it takes) sessions with the parents and two children's meetings.

And what would you do at these parent meetings? You want to give the parents the tools they need to be able to catechize their children. What is it that parents have to teach their children about first communion? Here's where the idea of a catechesis *modeled* on baptismal catechesis comes into play. Paragraph 75 of the RCIA says that in order to be fully catechized, the catechumens must have an appropriate understanding of the church's understanding of word, worship, community, and service. What you will prepare the parents to do is help their children understand these key elements of our tradition *in a way that is appropriate for a child* who is just beginning to understand his or her faith.

How do you know if the children have learned enough? Many parishes could ask that question of their traditional, text-based preparation programs and still not come up with a satisfactory answer. In a text-based program, children are sometimes considered "catechized" if they have come to a minimum number of classes and perhaps passed a written or oral exam.

In a process modeled on baptismal catechesis, it is likely that each candidate, along with his or her parents, would be interviewed by a member of the preparation team as part of a discernment process. The candidate, parents, and pastoral team would work together to determine if the candidate is ready to celebrate first communion. The discernment would center on the four key elements of the tradition. If the candidate is weak in one or more of these areas, he or she stays in the preparation process until his or her faith is strengthened accordingly.

This is a very broad stroke, just to give a hint about how you might begin to shift from a child-centered, classroom model of catechesis to an adult-centered, baptismal model of catechesis. The GDC lays out an extraordinary vision, and most of us will never fully accomplish the goals it sets forth. However, if we can take *some* steps toward the vision, our children will be able to build on what we've started. ("Ladies and gentlemen, the captain has turned off the fasten seatbelt sign. The aircraft is once again under control. We will be landing shortly.")

For discussion

- ☐ Is the primary catechetical effort in your community directed toward adults? What strategies can you and your brainstorming team devise to move the parish in that direction?
- ☐ What efforts are made to reach out to those who have not yet heard the Gospel? What strategies can you and your brainstorming team devise to strengthen those efforts?
- ☐ What discernment processes presently take place in your community? What additional discernment processes are required?

Doing Away With Our "Don't Touch" Theology

I grew up in a church that not only had a communion rail but also still had that white veil the altar boys flipped over the rail at communion time so communicants could place their hands under it and eliminate any possibility of having their sinful flesh come into contact with the Real Presence. I wanted more than anything to be an altar boy so I could flip that cloth with the same ease and flair that my acolyte-idols did. Alas, by the time I reached server age, the reforms of Vatican II had done away with both the majestic cloth and the rail.

What my boyhood liturgy did leave me with—and what Vatican II could never take away from me—was a lingering feeling every time I walk into a church that there are things there I should not touch. Mind you, I am a professional liturgist. I have studied and worked with these liturgical artifacts. I have analyzed and deconstructed their meanings. I can tell you the theological significance of most of them from the point of view of several different eras in church history. These things are almost as familiar and common to me as my name. Yet I was deeply catechized not to touch, and I still get butterflies when I handle something "holy."

As the person in charge of liturgical catechesis in your parish, that should worry you a little. Most Catholics in their 40s and older have the same sense of distance and unworthiness around things liturgical. Most liturgies and catechetical programs are designed and executed by us pre–Vatican II folks. Aren't you worried that we might be transmitting some of our pre–Vatican II "don't touch" theology to those who are following after us? I am.

Well, sometimes I am. Other times I think maybe these youngsters need to show a little more respect.

Maybe it wouldn't hurt if they thought twice before they stepped foot into the church, much less the *sanctuary*.

I have to catch myself when I start thinking this way. A "don't touch" theology implies there are keepers of the holy things who dispense them out to us as we need them. The holy things are not *ours*, and we cannot just walk around as if we own the place. It is the same feeling I have when I go to one of those high-end men's clothing stores, the kind of place where handkerchiefs start at about $40. I walk in there, and the keepers of the holy things *sense* I do not belong. They smile politely and say welcome to Gotbucks Clothier, but they know. And I know. And I pretend to look around—but I don't touch—and then I leave feeling a little unworthy.

We cannot catechize our children to feel that way. They have to be deeply catechized that they are made worthy by their baptism. Worthy to step into the church—anywhere in the church. Worthy to touch the holy things. Worthy to be active participants in the midst of the worshiping assembly.

As the chief catechist of the parish, it is important that you are aware of how the liturgy is catechizing or mis-catechizing the community. Those of us who were raised with a "don't touch" theology sometimes carry this over into the way we think about critiquing the liturgy. We don't think we are allowed to suggest changes and improvements because it is not for us to shape the "holy things."

If we do think that way, we have to get beyond it for the sake of those who are coming after us. Every church minister—especially those involved in catechesis—should be able to quickly identify several principles of good liturgy—principles upon which catechesis is based—and identify whether those principles are being well tended in a given celebration. Then, using these principles as a guide, we can critique any liturgy. Many things go into making liturgy work well, but no liturgy will work—nor will it catechize correctly—if the basics are not the first thing done well.

1st principle:
Active participation
of the assembly

The most basic principle is that liturgy is the work of the people. It does not belong to the keepers. It belongs to us. Making the liturgy overly complicated, changing it too frequently, doing too many new songs, prayers or actions are things that the keepers do that say "don't touch." A good pastoral team will strive to discover songs, prayers and actions the assembly can and will readily engage in and they will use those elements with great frequency.

It is by engaging in this active participation that the community becomes "educated" about the faith and about Jesus. According to the *General Directory of Catechesis* (85):

> Christ is always present in his Church, especially in "liturgical celebrations" (*Constitution on the Sacred Liturgy* 7). Communion with Jesus Christ leads to the celebration of his salvific presence in the sacraments, especially in the Eucharist. The Church ardently desires that all the Christian faithful be brought to that full, conscious and active participation which is required by the very nature of the liturgy (cf. CSL 14) and the dignity of the baptismal priesthood. For this reason, catechesis, along with promoting a knowledge of the meaning of the liturgy and the sacraments, must also educate the disciples of Jesus Christ "for prayer, for thanksgiving, for repentance, for praying with confidence, for community spirit, for understanding correctly the meaning of the creeds ..." (*General Catechetical Directory* [1971] 25b), as all of this is necessary for a true liturgical life.

"Prayer," "thanksgiving," "repentance," "praying with confidence," "community spirit" and "understanding correctly" are some of the "holy things" that go into making good liturgy. Catechists, and all who participate in the liturgy, must not be afraid to handle them and take ownership of them.

2nd principle:
Word and sacrament

Sunday liturgy and sacramental liturgies are always two-part celebrations of word and sacrament—usually Eucharist. Sometimes the keepers will let us take charge of the intercessions or the preparation of gifts or let us do something after communion. But these are not the central elements of the liturgy. Focus on catechizing and involving the assembly in Word and Eucharist. Make sure these two elements are clear, compelling and powerful. These are the key elements upon which you will base your catechetical efforts, and they need to be outstanding.

The simplest way to make the Liturgy of the Word a more truly catechetical event is to make sure the lectors in your community are excellent. Encourage the lectors to engage in regular training sessions and regular faith-sharing sessions throughout the liturgical year. A more difficult but also necessary step is to be sure the homilies in your parish are excellent. The members of the assembly are not to be let off the hook of active participation when it comes to the homily. They can be encouraged to give input and feedback to the homilists about the quality and content of the preaching they experience. The U.S. bishops, in their document *Fulfilled in Your Hearing: The Homily in the Sunday Assembly*, say (4):

> We believe that it is appropriate, indeed essential, to begin this treatment of the Sunday homily with the assembly rather than with the preacher of the homily .... Only when preachers know what their congregations want to hear will they be able to communicate what a congregation needs to hear. Homilists may indeed preach on what they understand to be the real issues, but if they are not in touch with what the people think are the real issues, they will very likely be misunderstood or not

heard at all. What is communicated is not what is said, but it is what is heard, and what is heard is determined in large measure by what the hearer needs or wants to hear.

3rd principle:
Liturgy leads to action

Every liturgy—every sacrifice of praise—commissions us to carry out the mission Jesus left us. God does not want our empty prayers. The effectiveness of our liturgies can be judged by how effectively our homes and neighborhoods are being transformed into microcosms of the kingdom. It is in the liturgy where we find Jesus most preeminently present. And the presence of Jesus is a revelation of justice (GDC 102):

> Jesus, in announcing the Kingdom, proclaims the justice of God: he proclaims God's judgment and our responsibility. The proclamation of this judgment, with its power to form consciences, is a central element in the Gospel, and Good News for the world: for those who suffer the denial of justice and for those who struggle to reinstate it; for those who have known love and existence in solidarity, because penance and forgiveness are possible, since in the Cross of Christ we all receive redemption from sin. The call to conversion and belief in the Gospel of the Kingdom—a Kingdom of justice, love and peace, and in whose light we shall be judged—is fundamental for catechesis.

> Jesus declares that the Kingdom of God is inaugurated in him, in his very person (cf. *Dogmatic Constitution on the Church* 3, 5). He reveals, in fact, that he himself, constituted as Lord, assumes the realization of the Kingdom until he consigns it, upon completion, to the Father when he comes again in glory (cf. *Redemptoris Missio* 16).

As the person in charge of catechesis in your parish, if you see to it that at least these three principles are applied consistently in your liturgical celebrations, the children of your community will never experience a "don't touch" theology of our faith. Instead, they will become active participants not only in the liturgy but also in the mission of the church to establish the kingdom of God's peace and justice.

For discussion

- ☐ What things in your worship space or in how you celebrate the liturgy seem to say "don't touch"? What is the theological understanding behind the "don't touch" message?
- ☐ Gather your brainstorming team. What are five ways you can more actively involve your community in Word and Eucharist? What are five ways you can help your community put into action in their homes the Word and Eucharist they celebrate?
- ☐ If the homilies in your parish are not excellent, what steps can you take to improve them? For example, can you gather a group of parishioners to read and study *Fulfilled in Your Hearing*? Can you invite the homilists to join you?

Catechesis in the Digital Age

Two things are changing the way we catechize. The first is the ubiquitousness of digital technology. The second is the emergence of liturgical catechesis (or baptismal catechesis) as the normative model for all catechesis.

When I say that digital technology is ubiquitous, you may not agree. Perhaps you don't use a computer much (or at all). No cell phone may have ever touched your ear. And your idea of an electronic organizer may be a battery-operated pencil sharpener and a desk lamp. Nevertheless, the digital age has changed your life. Besides all the hidden ways in which you use computers but may not be aware of it (just using an ordinary telephone, for example), most of those whom you seek to catechize are immersed in the digital culture. The times are changing, whether we want them to or not.

This is true of catechesis as well. The second change is the shift toward catechesis modeled upon the baptismal catechumenate. While not slavishly imitating the catechumenate, all catechesis should flow from and lead to the liturgy. The new *General Directory for Catechesis* points out that catechetical processes "frequently" have only "a weak and fragmentary link with the liturgy" (30). In the future, successful catechesis will have to recognize its intrinsic link to the liturgy.

Understanding the new digital culture is important. Children today are growing up with devices that help them manipulate their reality at will. Consider desktop computers. For you and me, a computer is a tool that helps us do our work better. It is a better typewriter or a better calculator than the one we used to use. Children of the digital generation (those born after 1980) don't think of computers as better tools. For them, computers are devices that help them understand the way the world works. Computers are important devices for helping young people understand

relationships, values, communication skills, culture, and art. Computers are not the only portals of such information for children, but increasingly, *any* of the methods whereby children learn about their world are coming to them in digital form.

For example, the toys your children play with as they grow up are recorded digitally when you buy them. They all have barcodes that get scanned into a computer. If you buy the toys with credit cards, that information can also be stored in a computer. Manufacturers can use this stored information to see what toys are selling well to what kinds of children and then create promotions directed at the parents of similar types of children in other areas. Those children will soon be playing with the same types of toys, and the "values" communicated by those toys will be communicated to your child's peers.

So before they are aware of what they are doing, children are interacting with their environment and, by that interaction, changing the reality of that environment. They shift the way the world around them looks and thinks and operates. As they grow older, their toys become more sophisticated and allow them to shape their realities more intentionally. The most significant thing you need to know about this is: The overarching value children learn these days is that they can interact and things will be different because of their interaction. Children today take it as a given that they can shape their world into something more responsive and interesting to them.

Catechesis for today's children

What this means for catechesis is that children will have difficulty in lesson-plan-based environments that

31

assume each person needs to learn the same thing in the same way at the same time. The next generation will also have difficulty accepting "universal" truths presented with dictums such as "As the church has always taught …" or "We've always done it that way." It's no that children don't believe in universal truths; they just understand the idea of "truth" as more flexible or more open to interpretation than do you and I. Our teaching—if it is going to have any credibility— needs to be done in such a way that young people can influence and shape the direction it takes. They need to be able to accommodate the catechesis to their own lives.

It is fortuitous, then, that the new *General Directory for Catechesis* promotes liturgical catechesis as the model for us to use. The primary source book for understanding the principles of liturgical catechesis is the *Rite of Christian Initiation of Adults*. While keeping in mind the GDC's caution not to slavishly imitate baptismal catechesis, every catechist should become familiar with paragraph 75 of the RCIA. If you design your catechetical program around the principles listed in that paragraph (actually several paragraphs), you will have an interactive and accommodating process. The RCIA calls for a "suitable catechesis" that is "accommodated" to the liturgy and the liturgical year. In other words, the liturgy *is the textbook* for all catechesis. By participating in—interacting with—the liturgy, young people will not only come to know the "dogmas and precepts" of the church but also "a profound sense of the mystery of salvation." Just as playing with their toys communicates values to them, playing with the liturgy will also communicate values, profound values, about the mysteries of the universe.

Paragraph 75 describes more principles of interaction. Digital children learn about reality by interacting with others. They interact the same ways you and I did as children, but they extend that interaction to a global presence through their facile use of e-mail, the internet and the world wide web. The old joke used to be that Baby Boomers had to get their children to program their VCRs for them. Now they have to get their grandchildren to build their web pages for them. The RCIA also envisions interaction with others as a principle of catechesis. "As they become familiar with the Christian way of life [they] are helped by the example and support of sponsors, godparents, and the entire Christian community." In the digital age, the phrase "entire Christian community" takes on a much more universal meaning than when the first drafts of the RCIA were composed in the 1970s. Children can connect with Christians all over the world within seconds.

Changing the world

The RCIA envisions a catechesis that leads to interaction with that world. Children and young people will be best served by a catechesis that teaches them "how to work actively with others to spread the Gospel and build up the Church by the witness of their lives and by professing their faith (See Vatican Council II, Decree on the Church's Missionary Activity *Ad gentes*, no. 14)." It is impossible to imagine how a predetermined, lesson-plan style of catechesis could accomplish so lofty a goal. In order to become fully involved in spreading the Gospel and witnessing to their faith, catechists will have to enter deeply into relationships with those they catechize. They will have to make themselves vulnerable and open their hearts to those to whom they minister. In other words, they have to be willing to let their interactions with children and young people change them. Children expect to be able to change the environments within which they interact. That includes us.

The GDC says that the goal of all catechesis is intimate communion with Jesus (80). The goal of catechesis is not to learn facts about God or religion. No test can verify that someone has achieved intimacy with Jesus. No attendance records can attest to the level of communion one has reached. *The only way* to know if someone is in communion and intimacy with Jesus is to be in intimate communion with the person yourself. Catechesis in the digital age demands new interactive skills that leave us open to new realities. Digital technology has changed our world forever and has changed those who are growing up in that new world. Old methods of catechesis will not find a comfortable fit with digital children.

The digital generation needs catechesis based on the baptismal catechumenate. They need catechesis that is interactive, participative, communicative and relational. They need catechesis that is based on and flows from the liturgy they celebrate and the worship in which they find intimacy with the Body of Christ.

For discussion

❑ Gather your brainstorming team. How strong is the link between your catechetical efforts and the liturgy? What are five strategies you can imagine to make the links between liturgy and catechesis more intrinsic?

❑ What are some strategies you can imagine to make your liturgical and catechetical process as interactive for children as the rest of the activities in their lives are?

❑ List three ways children can be encouraged to deepen their intimacy with Jesus through their digital and actual relationships. Can these three efforts become the focus of your catechetical efforts with children this year? Next year?

The Primary Task of Catechesis

My first attempt at being a catechist took place when I was a sophomore in high school. The local DRE gave me a student textbook and a corresponding teacher's book, patted me on the back and said with what was supposed to be a reassuring smile, "You'll do fine. It's all in the book." I had no idea what my task was or how I was supposed to do it.

You might be thinking, as I did back then, that the primary task of catechesis is something like handing on the faith or preparing people to celebrate the sacraments. Those are important tasks, but they are not the sort of thing identified by the *General Directory of Catechesis* as the *primary* task. The primary task of catechesis is the formation of the *catechists* in "the deep riches of the faith" (33).

Who are the catechists?

If our first task is to train the catechists, it might be helpful to know about whom we are talking. The GDC lists the following as catechists (222–230):

- parents—who are called the primary catechists of their families
- the bishop
- members of the clergy
- members of religious orders
- the laity

The group that receives the most attention in the GDC regarding their formation are the lay catechists. Indeed, all the laity are called, by our baptism, to be catechists. However, some of us received an additional interior call to serve in the ministry of catechist (231). I cannot recall any particular *interior* call, just the telephone call from the DRE impressing upon me my "Catholic duty" to volunteer. Nevertheless, I and all

those who find themselves in similar situations today are the particular kind of lay catechist that the GDC is most concerned with.

What does a catechist do?

In order to understand the formation process needed for these lay catechists, it is important to understand what a catechist is supposed to do. I learned what a catechist is supposed to do the hard way. Being a good student myself, I did what I thought my secular teachers had done to prepare me for learning. I read the teacher's manual, I took notes, I worked out a lesson plan, and I set down a three-month outline of the course material to cover. Then, diligently, Sunday after Sunday, I stood in front of my ferocious fifth graders, methodically covering each point the teacher's manual directed me to cover. They were, of course, bored to tears.

One Sunday I had to be away. Through the DRE, I arranged for a substitute. I called my designated sub several times but wasn't able to connect before I had to leave town. So I mailed her the teacher's manual, my lesson plan for the Sunday, and my three-month outline.

I wrote extensive notes to her about what she needed to cover in her allotted hour. When I returned the next Sunday, a grandmotherly woman met me at my room to return my materials. She thanked me for all my "suggestions" and then said, "I just prayed the Our Father with them and asked them what they thought that prayer meant to them. We had a wonderful time."

That's when I learned what the job of a catechist is. It is simply to first of all *communicate* (235). The GDC reminds us that, "In the catechetical process, the recipient must be an active subject, conscious and co-responsible, and not merely a silent, passive recipient" (167). For that to happen, catechists need to know how to enter into authentic dialog, authentic communication, so the person of Jesus can be revealed and made known.

Catechist formation

The first goal and purpose of formation, then, is to give the catechist skills in communication. The content of the communication is important. Catechists sometimes think of content as what is in the book—as I did with my fifth graders. My grandmotherly substitute knew that the "content" that was important was the experience and person of Jesus Christ. She asked, "When you pray, what does it mean to you?" When we enter into dialog with God, what happens in that encounter? What insights do we get? What is revealed? What is known from engaging in that process? How are we changed? What have we learned? The answers to these kinds of questions are the *content* that needs to be communicated. Being in communion—communication—with Jesus is the goal of all catechesis (80).

Formation of the catechist has to focus primarily on the skills needed to communicate the good news that Jesus is the revelation and sacrament of God for us. This might give some diocesan formation directors pause. With all good will, many diocesan programs are being set up to teach theology to catechists. These mini-schools sometimes take years to matriculate through, giving the catechist an academic background in salvation history, sacramental and moral theology, liturgy, canon law and the like.

Other programs move away from the school-model of catechist formation to something closer to what is envisioned by the GDC: "The *pedagogy* used in this formation [of catechists] is of fundamental importance. As a general criterion, it is necessary to underline the need for a coherence between the general pedagogy of formation of catechists and the pedagogy proper to the catechetical process. It would be very difficult for the catechist in his [or her] activity to improvise a style and a sensibility to which he [or she] had not been introduced during his [or her] own formation"

(237). In other words, the formation of the catechist should be modeled on the process used in the parish.

The catechetical process

So what does the parish catechetical process look like? It certainly doesn't (or shouldn't) look like what I tried to do with my fifth graders. Rather, it should look like the baptismal catechumenate (29, 59). The catechumenate model is not a classroom model, tied to text books and lesson plans. The catechumenal model looks like what my grandmotherly catechist did. She took worship experience common to the fifth graders (the Lord's Prayer) and called out their experience from them. If she was as skilled as I suspect she was, she then tied that experience into the framework of what the church believes about Jesus. In other words, by adapting herself to the particular experience of the fifth graders, she was able to communicate how Jesus was already a part of their experience.

The formation of catechists ideally follows the same model. A catechist formation process is ideally experiential, building on the common experience of the catechists, revealing to them ever deeper levels of Christ's presence. According to the GDC, "The christocentric purpose of catechesis, which emphasizes the communion of the convert with Jesus Christ, permeates all aspects of the formation of the catechists. … The formation of catechists is nothing other than an assistance for them in identifying with the living and actual awareness that the Church has of the Gospel, in order to make them capable of transmitting it in his name" (235–236).

This does not in any way imply that catechists should never participate in a systematic, academic study of the teachings of the church. It is only to say that such study cannot be a substitute for the primary formation they require.

Conclusion

It was a long time before I ever volunteered to be a catechist again. I had it fixed in my mind that being a catechist meant teaching the facts of the faith in a systematic format, contained in textbooks. I knew I hadn't learned my faith that way, and I felt inadequate trying to teach others about Jesus that way. It was not until I learned about the catechumenate process that I first felt "an additional interior call" to the ministry of catechist. That made sense to me. That was a process of mentoring, example, and apprenticeship similar to the way I had come to know Jesus and his mission. It was a way I thought I could effectively *communicate* what I believed.

It is a method that is effective not only for those searching for faith but for those who already have faith and want to deepen their faith. Living, flesh and blood people communicate. The Body of Christ communicates. Our primary task today is to find people willing to communicate Jesus to others and to form them to effectively do that.

For discussion

☐ Is the content of your catechetical program more focused on texts or on relationships? Can you and your team brainstorm three ways to shift the focus more to relationships over the next year?

☐ Observe the catechumenate process in your parish or another one. What are four things they do to communicate the message of Jesus? How can those things be adapted and used in the rest of the parish catechetical efforts?

☐ What is the formation process used for your catechists? Are they formed in a classroom model or a catechumenal-style process? What are the benefits and challenges of moving to a more catechumenal-style process?

What's Right — and Wrong — with Catechesis Today

Do you tell war stories? Catechists sometimes get wrapped up in talking to each other about the battles of trying to effectively catechize. Mostly this is a healthy way to vent emotions. Sometimes, however, it helps to get a broader perspective so we can see the joys as well as the struggles in our catechetical efforts.

What's right

The *General Directory for Catechesis* lists several things that are going right with catechesis (cf. 29). First the document notes that a great number of priests, religious, and laity are enthusiastic about catechesis. Take stock in your parish. Do you sense there are a great number of people who are enthusiastic about catechesis? Think of how many people you could identify in your parish as "enthusiastic" about catechesis. Is that number greater, smaller, or the same as it was five years ago? If the number is growing, your community is doing something right to raise the level of enthusiasm. If the number is stagnant or falling, what steps can you take over the next five years to increase enthusiasm?

The GDC also lists as a positive "the missionary character of contemporary catechesis." By this, the document means that catechesis is oriented toward conversion of hearts. The GDC notes that catechesis today engenders real faith on the part of catechumens and others to be catechized even though we live in a world that rejects the values of the Gospel. This success is due to "an acute awareness that catechesis must have a catechumenal style, as of integral formation rather than mere information." Does your parish catechesis fit that description? Are the catechumens and others in your catechetical process truly converted to the Gospel? Do the catechists in your community intuitively understand the difference between formation and information? Likely, that is the case in your parish. If not, what steps can you begin taking now so that in five years your process will reflect the successes the GDC sees taking place in most communities?

On a somewhat parallel track, the GDC also lists as a success the expanding role of adult catechesis in many communities. While there is still a ways to go, adult catechesis in many communities "appears to be a priority in the pastoral planning ...." You may find that to be true in your community because many parishes have worked hard over the last decade to put a higher priority on forming adults. If you think your community doesn't quite measure up to the standards you'd like, what will you be able to put in place over the next five years to move your community to a better place? The U.S. bishops have recently released a plan to help parishes in this effort: *Our Hearts Were Burning Within Us: A Pastoral Plan for Adult Faith Formation in the United States.* A liturgical critique of the plan appears on the Resource Publications, Inc. website (www.rpinet.com/ml/2706hrts.html).

What's wrong

The GDC is not Pollyannaish, however. It recognizes that there are problems that need attention (30). Even though catechesis is to be understood as "an initiation and apprenticeship in the entire Christian life," catechists do not fully understand that notion. The GDC sees most catechetical activity focusing almost exclusively on Scripture without sufficient reference to church teaching. "The ecclesial nature of catechesis, in this case, appears less clearly; the interrelation of Sacred Scripture, Tradition and the Magisterium, each according to 'its proper mode' (*Dei Verbum* 10c) does not yet harmoniously enrich a catechetical transmission of the faith."

Another difficulty is that many times the humanity of Christ is emphasized without a balanced presentation of Jesus' divinity. Or in other communities, the emphasis is placed almost exclusively on Christ's divinity.

The GDC then lists deficiencies in the content of a "proliferation of catechisms and texts," which include a need for more moral formation, more on church history, and more on social teaching.

Even though catechesis cannot be separated from the liturgy, "the practice of catechetics testifies to a weak … link with the liturgy: limited attention to liturgical symbols …, catechetical courses with little or no connection with the liturgical year; the marginalization of liturgical celebrations in catechetical programs."

Multiculturalism can sometimes be another hurdle because it is difficult to know how to communicate the Gospel to people of diverse cultures in a way that makes sense to them and really does sound like good news. Most cultures today are infused with a "scientific mentality" (20). This mentality, no matter what culture it finds itself in, has a profound effect on traditional ways of thinking. Almost everywhere, people are influenced by the scientific and experimental method. The GDC recognizes that among our efforts at trying to inculturate our catechesis into traditional cultures, we must also work at promoting a catechesis that complements the scientific mentality without remaining captive to it. If we are to succeed in knowing what it means to be humans who struggle to believe, we must incorporate into our catechesis "some other method of knowing" alongside our scientific method.

In many places there still is insufficient formation of the laity for missionary activity. This weakness exists even though formation for mission is a fundamental task of catechesis. The GDC identifies the mission as follows: "Jesus Christ, after his Resurrection together with the Father sent the Holy Spirit in order that he might accomplish from within the work of salvation and that he might animate his disciples to continue the mission to the whole world" (34).

The missionary activity for which we must form the laity is the "work of salvation" begun by Jesus and continued on in the disciples. The "work of salvation," according to the *Catechism of the Catholic Church*, "is none other than to make [humankind] share in the communion between the Father and the Son in their Spirit of love" (850).

Not all of these weaknesses will appear in every catechetical program, but almost every parish probably has at least one weak link. It might be a useful exercise to ask the catechists of the parish if they can identify any of these difficulties as issues for your community. If there are more than a couple, perhaps you might decide collectively to prioritize one or two to focus on improving over the next five years.

Challenges

The GDC has its own list of priorities for the universal church. This might be another checklist to use when you are trying to gain perspective about the catechesis in your parish. In order to strengthen our catechetical efforts, the GDC lays out five challenges (33):

- Catechesis today needs to serve the church's efforts at evangelization, especially emphasizing its missionary character.
- Catechesis should be focused on those who are its "privileged recipients": children, adolescents, young people and adults.
- Using the patristics as a model, catechesis should "form the personality of the believer and therefore be a true and proper school of Christian pedagogy."
- Our catechetical efforts need to clearly promote the essential mysteries of our faith, especially the mystery of the Trinity with Christ as the center of our belief.
- Finally, catechesis needs to focus on its primary task: "the preparation and formation of catechists in the deep riches of the faith."

With all that in mind, allow me to tell you a "war story." My community began a new catechetical effort about four years ago. Our goals were to focus mostly on the first two challenges suggested by the GDC. We sought to serve the church's efforts at evangelization by focusing our entire program on bringing people "not only in touch, but in communion and intimacy with Jesus." We also intended from the beginning to focus on the "privileged recipients," which includes all God's people, no matter what age. So from the beginning our process has spanned from nursery level to adult, and we made a commitment to continue our process year-round. The "battle" in this war story is we have never had enough catechists to cover all these age groups, 52 weeks of the year. But most weeks, through creative juggling, we have managed to avoid total disaster. Just by seeing how committed the catechists are to making our fledgling process work helps the participants feel a greater, more intimate connection to the Body of Christ. By next year—year five—we will have mostly met our first two challenges. It will soon be time for us to choose a couple more goals to meet in the following five years—and time to share a few more war stories before moving on to new battles.

For discussion

- ❏ Gather your brainstorming team or your parish catechists. List on a white board the positive advancements and weaknesses of catechesis as described in the GDC. Identify the three strongest "positives" in your parish. How can you keep those going?
- ❏ Identify the three greatest weaknesses of catechesis in your parish. What can you do over the next one to five years to turn those into positives?
- ❏ Look at the five challenges presented in the GDC (33). Which two of these challenges could your community tackle over the next five years?

Catechists As Evangelists

If you asked your catechists, "Do you consider yourself an evangelist?" how would they reply?

The *General Directory for Catechesis* says the process of evangelization is structured in stages or "essential moments" (49):

a) missionary activity directed toward nonbelievers
b) initial catechetical activity
c) pastoral activity directed toward the Christian faithful of mature faith

Catechesis is a "moment" within this process of evangelization. Relying on the document *Catechesi Tradendae*, the GDC notes that there are activities within the whole process of evangelization that prepare for catechesis and activities that derive from it (63).

Primary catechesis

The first of these evangelistic activities is the proclamation of the word toward nonbelievers. The primary proclamation is distinct from catechesis in the pure sense of each activity. However, "in pastoral practice it is not always easy to define the boundaries of these activities. Frequently, many who present themselves for catechesis truly require genuine conversion" (62). So the catechist must first of all be concerned with the genuine conversion of those she seeks to catechize.

Initiatory catechesis

The next activity of evangelization is more strictly speaking "catechesis." "Converts, by means of 'a period of formation, an apprenticeship in the whole Christian life' (*Ad gentes* 14), are initiated into the mystery of salvation and an evangelical style of life" (63). This "initiatory catechesis" is the foundation for all Christian life that will follow. The GDC lists characteristics of this "essential moment" in the process of evangelization (67):

- a comprehensive and systematic formation in the faith
- this comprehensive formation includes more than instruction: it is an apprenticeship of the entire Christian life, it is a "complete Christian initiation" (CT 21)
- a basic and essential formation, centered on what constitutes the nucleus of Christian experience, the most fundamental certainties of the faith and the most essential evangelical values

The GDC summarizes all that initiatory catechesis should be:

As it is formation for the Christian life it comprises but surpasses mere instruction. Being essential, it looks to what is "common" for the Christian, without entering into disputed questions nor transforming itself into a form of theological investigation. Finally, being initiatory, it incorporates into the community, which lives, celebrates and bears witness to the faith. It fulfills, at once, initiatory, educational and instructional functions. This inherent richness in the Cathechumenate of nonbaptized adults should serve to inspire other forms of catechesis (68).

Ongoing catechesis

Initiatory catechesis serves as a bridge to the third evangelistic activity, continuing or ongoing education in the faith. This continuing catechesis uses many different forms. The GDC lists them as (71):

- the exploration of Scripture
- an understanding of current events from a Christian perspective
- liturgical catechesis, which must be regarded as an "eminent kind of catechesis" (CT 23)
- occasional catechesis that seeks to interpret the circumstances of our lives
- systematic catechesis, which may also be called "perfective catechesis"

This ongoing catechesis is to be closely linked with initiatory catechesis in order to give an authentic foundation to the evangelizing activity of the church. It is also important "that the catechesis of children and young people, permanent catechesis and the catechesis of adults should not be separate watertight compartments (CT 45c)" (GDC 72).

Making it work

So what does all this mean for your community? Most importantly, it means that we cannot think of catechesis primarily in terms of classrooms, lesson plans, and adult education meetings. Catechists are not in the first place teachers of fact; they are teachers of a lifestyle. They are essential components of the church's mission to evangelize. Catechists may not usually be called upon to provide the "primary proclamation of the Gospel (CT 19)" (cf. GDC 61), but they are nevertheless key people in the mission of evangelization.

To make the vision of the GDC come alive, it will be important to train catechists in multiple skills. The evangelizing mission of the church will not be realized if catechists remain in their "separate watertight compartments." A children's catechist will have to be able to catechize the parents of those children. An adult catechist will have to be able to evangelize the husband or sister of the "hearer" in her

Thursday night faith-sharing group. An RCIA catechist will have to know how to provide ongoing catechesis for the sponsors of the catechumens.

This does not mean catechists have to have master's degrees in theology. It means they have to know in their bones what the goal is. The goal is to evangelize. The church exists to evangelize. The church exists to enable the member of the Body to go out into the world and proclaim the good news that Jesus can save us all from darkness and loneliness.

The job of the catechist is to teach whomever he comes in contact with how to do that. It is the job of the catechist to teach all the faithful—or the potentially faithful—how to be an evangelizer. Jesus, of course, is our model: "As an evangelizer, Christ first of all proclaims a kingdom, the kingdom of God; and this is so important that, by comparison, everything else becomes 'the rest'" (*On Evangelization in the Modern World* 8).

We can judge the effectiveness of the catechist by how effectively those in her charge cause the people around them to take notice of Gospel values:

> Above all the Gospel must be proclaimed by witness. Take a Christian or a handful of Christians who, in the midst of their own community, show their capacity for understanding and acceptance, their sharing of life and destiny with other people, their solidarity with the efforts of all for whatever is noble and good. Let us suppose that, in addition, they radiate in an altogether simple and unaffected way their faith in values that go beyond current values, and their hope in something that is not seen and that one would not dare to imagine. Through this wordless witness these Christians stir up irresistible questions in the hearts of those who see how they live: Why are they like this? Why do they live in this way? What or who is it that inspires them? Why are they in our midst? Such a witness is already a silent proclamation of the Good News and a very powerful and effective one. Here we have an initial act of evangelization (*On Evangelization* 21).

Providing effective catechesis

A mastery of facts about our faith is not first of all essential for catechists. What is essential is that they be faith-filled people. What will identify them as effective catechists is not their ability to turn out children who can recite the ten commandments and the seven sacraments. It will instead be their ability to create within the community a sense of mission to go out and proclaim good news to the poor and love for one another. This goal must become so important to them that everything else is considered "the rest."

It is clear, then, that catechist "training" begins first of all with the trainer. Those in charge of catechist recruitment and formation must be evangelists themselves. They must be willing to make the proclamation of the kingdom their first and final priority. They must exude a sense of mission that is contagious and compelling. If you are that kind of leader, and someone asks your catechists, "Do you consider yourself an evangelist?", you will know even before they are asked what their response will be: "Of course. Aren't we all?"

For discussion

☐ As a trainer of catechists, what is your first priority in your own ministry of catechesis? Do your priorities come through in your training processes?

☐ Who in your parish would you identify as an excellent catechist? What are some of the multiple skills that person uses to catechize? How can other catechists be mentored to develop similar skills?

☐ How are catechists in your parish evaluated? What processes and questions do you use to gauge their effectiveness? Do all your catechists know what you consider to be an "effective" catechist?

Artful Catechesis

Catechesis, we all know, is a ministry of the word. Sometimes, however, we take that to mean catechesis is a ministry of words. It is not. Catechesis is much more a ministry of images. Even when we use words in our ministry, we are called to teach as Jesus did—using stories, word-paintings, images, and examples.

We know that "in the beginning was the Word" (Jn 1:1). But that word was not words. It was the word of an artist creating an image (in the image of God he created them; male and female he created them [Gn 1:27]). One liturgist imagines the creation story as a flow of paint and color brushing creation into being every time God "said" something.

The job of the catechist, said Karl Rahner, is not to pump religion into people. It is to draw faith out of them. Faith is not a set of propositions (more words) that can be proved; it is an ardent response to God's self-revelation. It is our "I love you, too" back to God. A catechist seeking to draw out a faith response would be well served by making use of the arts, particularly visual arts, as a tool to help children and adults explore the movement of God's spirit within them.

In fact, some truths of our faith can perhaps only be expressed in art forms—or at least they are best expressed that way. "But truth can also find other complementary forms of human expression, above all when it is a matter of evoking what is beyond words: the depths of the human heart, the exaltations of the soul, the mystery of God" (*Catechism of the Catholic Church* 2500).

Perhaps we resist using images, relying more on words, because images can be more difficult to manage, are more open to varied interpretations, and are not easily locked into definitions that can be written into catechisms and creeds. The great advantage of using visual art, however, is the very quality of ambiguity. Visual art forms provide many facets for the faithful

to gaze upon and enter into the experience. And it does not need to be "religious" art to serve this function. Pope John Paul II says in his 1999 *Letter to Artists*:

> 6. Every genuine artistic intuition goes beyond what the senses perceive and, reaching beneath reality's surface, strives to interpret its hidden mystery. The intuition itself springs from the depths of the human soul, where the desire to give meaning to one's own life is joined by the fleeting vision of beauty and of the mysterious unity of things. All artists experience the unbridgeable gap which lies between the work of their hands, however successful it may be, and the dazzling perfection of the beauty glimpsed in the ardor of the creative moment: what they manage to express in their painting, their sculpting, their creating is no more than a glimmer of the splendor which flared for a moment before the eyes of their spirit.

What are some ways catechists can make use of the arts in order to catechize? There are two methods to explore. One we will call the "contemplative method." The contemplative method is analogous to going to a museum to view art and allow it to move us. The experience of *viewing* the art is one of revelation—of the artist; of the hidden, mysterious experience behind the art; and of ourselves as we become engaged in the artwork.

The other method is one we can call the "liturgical method." While fine art can lead to a religious experience, that is not necessarily its express purpose— even if it is "religious art." Liturgical art, on the other hand, is more like the finely woven baskets of native Americans or the elegantly designed furniture of the Bauhaus craft movement. Liturgical art is not meant merely to be contemplated; it is meant to be used for something.

Contemplative method

This method can be used with any piece of fine art, poetry, music, or great literature. The goal is to expose the participants to the art and draw out from them their reflection on it in the context of the Christian story. Maureen Gallagher describes the process in her book, *The Art of Catechesis*. Her description, however, relates specifically to reflection on a story. It is adapted here to presume a reflection on a painting or a copy of a painting. You could further adapt the method to any art form.

1. Find an artist or style of art you particularly enjoy (e.g., French Impressionism), and look at several different paintings. (See the August 2000 *Ministry & Liturgy* for 46 websites that deal with art.)
2. Find several works that interest you, disturb you, raise your emotions, make you smile, make you sad, etc. Sometimes you may have to make decisions based on the age level of your group. However, don't sell the younger children short by choosing only cute or simple pieces.
3. Ask yourself how you might introduce the work. What drew you to it? What did you like about it? What moved you about it?
4. Ask yourself if there are any connections between the art and Scripture stories. Sometimes an art piece is very scriptural but does not reveal itself as such on a first viewing. Look for "lines" in the painting that form a cross. Look to see what images the artist has placed "on the cross." Look for birth and death themes. Look for harvest themes. The more abstract the painting, the more possibilities there are for multiple interpretations. That all by itself may lead to a catechetical moment. How can one person in the group see "death" in the painting while another is convinced it is all about "life"? Is there a connection between those opposed interpretations and our individual understandings of God?
5. Can you list five discussion questions for each work you choose that would lead the participants to reflect on the meaning of the painting? Can you

think of at least one follow-up question for each of those questions that might lead them to make a connection between the painting and an experience of God?
6. What might be the advantages and disadvantages of using the works you have chosen for a catechetical session?

Liturgical method

Environment and Art in Catholic Worship is an excellent resource for understanding the role of art in the liturgy. The document makes clear that art used in the liturgy carries all the same burdens of fine art to reveal the handstamp of the artist and the mystery of the creator within. However, the piece carries the additional task of needing to serve an appropriate function within the liturgy.

One difficulty with focusing on liturgical art is that our artistic sense in many liturgical spaces is quite diminished. The church in the United States and in much of the West is just now emerging from an era in which function, not beauty, was the dominating criterion. There was even a sense of pride in being able to reduce our liturgical symbols and art forms to their bare minimum to demonstrate our thriftiness and ingenuity. If your parish is still struggling to understand the role and necessity of beauty in its liturgical art forms, it might be useful to spend several sessions on contemplative art, choosing recognized masterpieces as your examples. After some exposure to the role of art *generally* in our lives and in the life of the world, it might be easier to make the point that our liturgical art would want to strive for the same kind of quality. (To view samples of some of the finest liturgical art being produced today, see the Visual Arts Awards issues of *Ministry & Liturgy*.)

In any case, a liturgical method might look like the following:

1. Either as part of a catechetical session or on your own, list the primary symbols we use in the liturgy and the sacraments. They will be things like bread, oil, water, book, etc. There will be other symbols that come to mind as well, such as colors, garments, banners, flowers, etc. Try to distinguish which are *primary* symbols and which are *secondary*.

"Secondary" symbols need to be beautiful as well, but it would be best to begin your reflections with primary symbols.

2. Having chosen a liturgical "art piece" or symbol, ask the participants to identify all the things they "see" in the symbol. Their first responses will be somewhat simple and obvious. What kinds of questions can you ask to invite them to see more deeply into the piece or symbol?

3. What does the use of that symbol in the liturgy say to the participants about the use of similar objects in their homes? For example, do they ever think of the bread of Eucharist being like the bread on their dinner tables? What connections are there between the "art forms" of the liturgy and the "functional forms" of daily life?

4. What kinds of questions can you ask to draw out how the participants understand the art or symbol to be a revelation of themselves? Of the community? Of God?

5. What connections can be made—by you or by them—between the use of the symbol in the liturgy and the way we choose to live our lives after the liturgy has ended? Does the use of the symbol have any "conversion" effect on us? Are we different from having used it?

For discussion

☐ Gather your brainstorming team and read together Pope John Paul II's *Letter to Artists*. List three things the pope's letter inspires you to do to make your catechetical process more artful.

☐ Read again the adaptation of the contemplative method of drawing out faith responses to a painting. How could you adapt the process to apply to classical music? To sculpture? To textiles? To architecture? To dance?

☐ Read again the adaptation of the liturgical method of drawing out faith responses to visual elements of the liturgy. How could you adapt the process to apply to musical, aural, or tactile elements?

Diagram for Catechesis

The GDC tells us, "Catechesis is an essentially ecclesial act. The true subject of catechesis is the Church which, continuing the mission of Jesus ..., is sent to be the teacher of the faith." The church (that's you and me and all the baptized) "transmits the faith in an active way; she sows it in the hearts of catechumens and those to be catechized so as to nourish their profoundest experience of life" (78).

Their *profoundest* experience of life? Perhaps that may not be the case in your parish, but it is not unreasonable to hope that *would become* the case. In striving to connect catechesis to profound experience, it helps to remember that the model for all catechesis is the baptismal catechumenate (59). If we center all our catechetical activity on the processes involved in bringing the unbaptized and uncatechized to faith, then the catechumenate itself becomes "a center of deepening catholicity and a ferment of ecclesial renewal" (78).

Think about why this must be true. For those who are catechized, their conversion to faith was, indeed, the profoundest of experiences. However, all of us know of people who have been subjected to catechetical instruction who have not had the initial conversion experience necessary to allow that instruction to take root. For them, catechesis is *not* a nourishment of "their profoundest experience of life" but merely a distraction. If we take the vision of the *Rite of Christian Initiation of Adults* seriously, it will be necessary for all those in the parish who are "catechized" to be actively involved in bringing the uncatechized to faith. We do this by example:

> The initiation of catechumens is a gradual process that takes place within the community of the faithful. By joining the catechumens in reflecting on the value of the paschal mystery and by renewing their own conversion, the faithful provide an example that will help the catechumens to obey the holy Spirit more generously (RCIA 4).

For that reason, the GDC tells us the *object* of catechesis is *Jesus*: "'The definitive aim of catechesis is to put people not only in touch, but also in communion and intimacy, with Jesus Christ' (*Catechesi Tradendae* 5)." The bulk of our efforts in catechesis, therefore, is directed toward those who are just coming to faith to help them "solidify and mature this first adherence" to Jesus. The majority of our time and energy in catechesis should be "to help those who have just converted ... 'to know his "mystery," the kingdom of God proclaimed by him, the requirements and comments contained in his Gospel message, and the paths that he has laid down for anyone who wishes to follow him' (CT 20c)" (80).

So how do you help those who need to be catechized to come to communion and intimacy with Jesus? The GDC makes the obvious point that you do it the same way *Jesus* brought his disciples to communion and intimacy (84):

- He made known to them the different dimensions of the kingdom of God.
- He taught them to pray.
- He prepared them for mission.

This leads us to six fundamental tasks of catechesis (GDC 85–86):

1. Promoting knowledge of the faith
2. Liturgical education
3. Moral formation
4. Teaching to pray
5. Education for community life
6. Missionary invitation

You will recognize that these tasks correlate exactly with the tasks involved in catechizing the catechumens (cf. RCIA 75).

Promoting knowledge of the faith

The disciples of Jesus will yearn to know the whole truth about Jesus and will long to deepen their knowledge of Tradition and Scripture. The GDC draws a parallel to our love for Jesus and our love for another human being. When we love someone, we want to know everything about that person. Our knowledge of that person comes gradually as we deepen our relationship. Our knowledge of the faith grows as we deepen our relationship with Jesus and his church.

Liturgical education

Communion with Christ leads to a celebration of that communion. In looking at our corporate celebration—our liturgical worship—the Second Vatican Council identified, as the aim to be considered before all else, the full, conscious and active participation by all the faithful in the liturgy (cf. *Constitution on the Sacred Liturgy* 14). Most of us learned about liturgy by doing liturgy. The GDC says we are to use the baptismal catechumenate as our model, and that means learning about liturgy by doing good liturgy— not by sitting in a class *about* liturgy.

Moral formation

Another dimension of the kingdom that Jesus shared with his disciples is the radical vision of equality, justice, and love that God extends to all of creation. Jesus shared this vision in every action of his ministry, but it is distilled most clearly in the Sermon on the Mount, in which Jesus "takes up the [Ten Commandments], and impresses upon it the spirit of the beatitudes" (85).

Teaching to pray

"When catechesis is permeated by a climate of prayer, the assimilation of the entire Christian life reaches its summit," according to GDC 85. "This … is especially necessary when … those to be catechized … feel weak or when they discover the mysterious action of God in their lives." Like the liturgy, prayer is learned by doing. Those of us who know how to pray show those to be catechized how to pray.

Education for community life

GDC 86 refers to the education for community life as an "apprenticeship" that calls for the following attitudes:

- a simple and humble spirit
- care for the least among us
- particular care for the alienated among us
- loving correction
- common prayer
- mutual forgiveness
- fraternal love, which embraces all the other attitudes

The GDC notes that our community is not restricted to Roman Catholics; catechesis "encourages fraternal attitudes toward members of other Christian churches and ecclesial communities."

Missionary initiation

"The evangelical attitudes which Jesus taught his disciples when he sent them on mission," continues GDC 86, "are precisely those which catechesis must nourish":

- seek out lost sheep (Who are those in our community who feel lost and rejected?)

- proclaim and heal at the same time (How can we be with people who are in pain and at the same time be models of Christ?)
- be poor (How do the choices about what we purchase—both as a parish and as individuals—reflect Gospel values?)
- know how to accept rejection and persecution (Do we feel secure in career and social choices that reflect the Gospel?)
- place trust in God (Are we at peace, even in difficult times?)
- expect no reward (Do we serve in order to be recognized, or are we content with anonymous service?)

Final observations

What Jesus did seems simple enough. However, his teaching was filled with layers of meaning. His method had a hidden complexity to it. Sometimes the complexity can seem daunting. However, most of the elements of catechesis are interwoven with the other elements. Each separate task, in a way, contains elements of and realizes the others. "One task echos the other: knowledge of the faith prepares for mission; the sacramental life gives strength for moral transformation" (87).

It is important, too, to remember that Jesus did not send the disciples off to school. He used their own life experience to help them come to faith. So, after wandering around the countryside with Jesus, living life with him, watching him heal, seeing him pray, sharing meals with him, Jesus is finally able to say to the disciples, "Who do you say that I am?" Peter, now profoundly converted, can answer confidently, "You are the Christ." Realizing that is a profound experience.

For discussion

- Gather your brainstorming team. Describe some of the most profound experiences of your lives. Have those experiences had an impact on your faith lives?
- Discuss the place where the bulk of your catechetical efforts are directed. How close are you to the goal set out by the GDC that the bulk of our efforts be directed toward those just coming to faith? How can you move closer?
- Discuss the six fundamental tasks of catechesis. What are you doing well? What needs to be improved?

A Model for Catechesis

The *General Directory for Catechesis* mandates that all catechesis be modeled on the baptismal catechumenate (59). Some have suggested it is not possible to turn all our parishioners into catechumens and herd them into structures that were meant for the unbaptized. Such a fear is unfounded. The GDC itself says the catechumenal model is not to be "slavishly" imitated (91); rather, the catechumenate process is meant to inspire and inform all other types of catechesis.

The structure of the catechumenate

The GDC summarizes the intent of paragraph 19 of the *Rite of Christian Initiation of Adults* by noting that "good catechesis is always done in steps" (88). This is a key element of the catechumenal structure that must inspire the way other forms of catechesis are accomplished. In the baptismal catechumenate, there are four stages—each stage associated with a level of faith in the catechumen. The stages are:

- the *precatechumenate* — an opportunity for exploring the beginnings of faith
- the *catechumenate* — a time for nurturing one's faith and growing in understanding and acceptance of conversion
- the time of *purification and enlightenment* — usually associated with Lent, this is a time of intense reflection, centered on conversion, in preparation for initiation
- the time of *mystagogy* — usually associated with the Easter season, a time to experience what it means to fully participate with the Christian community by means of "pertinent" catechesis.

"These stages, which reflect the wisdom of the great catechumenal tradition, also inspire the gradual nature of catechesis" (89).

Finding our inspiration

The GDC makes clear that our mandate to evangelize the world "is the paradigm of all the Church's missionary activity" (90; see also Session 6 of this book). For that reason, the baptismal catechumenate, which is joined to that mission, is the model for our catechizing activity: "It is therefore helpful to underline those elements of the catechumenate which must inspire contemporary catechesis and its significance" (90). The GDC cautions, however, that there is a fundamental difference between catechumens and the faithful who are to be catechized, "between *pre-baptismal* catechesis and … *post-baptismal* catechesis."

The GDC then identifies the following five points of inspiration derived from the baptismal catechumenate (91):

1. **Initiation is the central activity of the church.** All our parish structures, including post-baptismal catechesis, are to be oriented toward evangelizing and initiating new members into the mission of Jesus.
2. **The baptismal catechumenate is everyone's responsibility.** If *pre-baptismal* catechesis is the responsibility of the entire community, the implication for the catechist is that *post-baptismal* catechesis is also the responsibility of the entire community. This does not mean everyone in the parish needs to become a formal catechist. It does mean that post-baptismal catechesis should be

primarily directed toward helping the faithful to live *more* faithfully so that they will catechize by their example.

3. **The baptismal catechumenate is permeated by the paschal mystery.** The Easter Vigil is our preeminent celebration of the paschal mystery. The implication for catechists is that the Easter Vigil should be the source and goal of all catechesis in the parish. An interesting discussion among the catechists in your parish might center on the question of what catechesis oriented toward the Easter Vigil would look like. How would first communion preparation be different? How would RENEW groups be different? How would Sunday homilies (a primary source of catechesis) be different?

4. **The baptismal catechumenate is a place where inculturation happens.** Catechumens are welcomed into the church with all their cultural background and history. Because the Son of God was made incarnate in a concrete time and place—and that cultural background was part and parcel of his identity as our savior—new Christians are likewise called to see the hand of God in their own cultural background. The implication for catechists is that the various cultures of all the faithful in the parish are places in which God's word has taken hold in various and rich ways. The challenge for the catechist is to listen to how that word is expressed and reflect it back in such a way that it becomes good news for everyone in the parish. For example, the catechist might be sensitive to how Latin American devotional practices can inform the ways in which people of Western-European descent understand how God works in their lives.

5. **The baptismal catechumenate is a process of formation.** We have seen that the catechumenate is structured in stages. The goal of the catechumenate is to appropriately form the catechumens at each stage of their faith development. Faith development continues to happen in stages *after* baptism. The implication for catechists is that post-baptismal catechesis must continue to happen in stages. Catechists will need to begin to think more about *levels of faith development* rather than age or grade levels. A one-size-fits-all catechesis will not do. Catechists must think creatively about how to communicate concepts appropriate to whatever stage of development the member of the faithful finds him or herself in.

Roadblocks

Some of the difficulty in fully implementing a style of catechesis inspired by the baptismal catechumenate might be due to some roadblocks we erect for ourselves or that we perceive others to have erected. See if any of these ring true in your parish:

- **If we don't catechize the children before they're (fill in an age), we'll lose them.** Even the people who make this kind of statement don't really believe it. How often have we heard confirmation referred to as the "graduation sacrament"? We compel young people to participate in a minimum number of classes so they can celebrate a sacrament—confirmation in this example. Those who choose to comply often leave our parishes shortly after. They are less catechized about the lifelong formation process required by the paschal mystery and more catechized about the minimalist nature of church participation.

- **Parents are not qualified to catechize their children.** Most catechists will agree that parents are *supposed to be* the primary catechists for their children. However, few will agree that they actually are. Sometimes we are never quite sure the parents will be able to teach their children things like the Ten Commandments or the moral positions of the church. The simple truth is, if parents are not able to impart the basics of the faith to their children, catechists—who have the children for perhaps an hour a week—will not be very successful in "making up" for what the parents lack. Our catechetical efforts, again following the model of the catechumenate, are to be primarily directed toward adults and not to children.

- **Adults will not come to adult education sessions.** The catechumenate shows this is simply not the case. On average, 160,000 adults have joined the church through the catechumenal process every year for the last five years. It is true that it is difficult to get adults to participate in adult education classes at church. As we've seen, however, a catechumenal model is not oriented toward the classroom. It is oriented toward the lives of the participants, the liturgy and catechetical reflection on how the liturgy connects to people's everyday lives. That kind of process is attractive.

- **A catechesis that relies primarily on the liturgy does not catechize fully enough.** Again, the catechumenate shows this to be untrue. People who join the church through the catechumenate are often better formed and informed about their faith than cradle Catholics who received most of their catechesis in a classroom format. In the course of the liturgical year the whole of salvation history and the requirements for living a Christian life are celebrated. A well-trained catechist will be able to easily connect our central doctrines to both the liturgical celebrations of the year and the lives of the faithful.

The church is calling us to adapt our catechetical efforts to take more inspiration from the baptismal catechumenate with good reason. The baptismal catechumenate is our most successful catechetical reform since the Second Vatican Council. We would do well, says the GDC, "to draw inspiration from 'this preparatory school for the Christian life' (*General Catechetical Directory* (1971) 130), and to allow [ourselves] to be enriched by those principal elements which characterize the catechumenate" (91).

For discussion

- Gather your brainstorming team. In what ways is your catechetical process inspired by the baptismal catechumenate? List one thing you can do to improve how your community does each of the five points of inspiration listed in the GDC (91).
- What are some of the stages of postbaptismal faith you've experienced? In what ways can you shape your catechetical processes to account for different levels of faith?
- Do you experience any of the roadblocks listed here? What other roadblocks do you experience? Identify at least one strategy to deal with each roadblock.

Inculturation

A key to understanding how to implement liturgical catechesis is understanding the process of inculturation. Catechesis cannot be effective if the Gospel message is not presented in a way that sounds like "good news" to the hearers. That means the Gospel must be proclaimed not only in a language that can be understood but also in a cultural context that is integral and intelligible to the hearers. Inculturation stands in contrast to globalization (or, in an earlier era, colonization).

"The church has to choose between inculturation and globalization," according to Pablo Richard, director of the Department of Ecumenical Investigation in San Jose, Costa Rica. "The church's catholicity can only be established in defense of life, of the spirit and of the cultures of the peoples who are oppressed and excluded by Western and modern globalization. Today, the church's catholicity faces the challenge of confronting a tradition that is still alive, a tradition of globalization that is ecclesial, Eurocentric, patriarchal, authoritarian and hostile to the body" (Pablo Richard, "Inculturation Defends Human, Cosmic Life," *National Catholic Reporter* [December 19, 1997]).

The church must choose because globalization is the imposition of a foreign culture on an already existing one. The church has been guilty of this in the past and could be in danger of continuing along the path of "ecclesial, Eurocentric, patriarchal, authoritarian" globalization. Nevertheless, the church's goal is to make true inculturation of the gospel a reality.

"'Inculturation' of the faith," says the *General Directory for Catechesis*," … is a profound and global process and a slow journey. It is not simply an external adaptation designed to make the Christian message more attractive or superficially decorative. On the contrary, it means the penetration of the deepest strata of persons and peoples by the Gospel which touches them deeply, 'going to the very center and roots' (*Evangelii Nuntiandi* 20) of their cultures" (109).

Making inculturation happen is not easy. It's long, slow, often frustrating work. It requires a suspension of prejudice about the relative efficiency or superiority of systems we've invested much of our lives in perfecting. If we are convinced our way is the only way (or the best way), we are in danger of promoting a catechesis that relies more on the principles of globalization than on inculturation.

Four tasks for inculturation

The GDC lists four different concrete tasks for catechists seeking to inculturate the faith.

• Catechists must first of all be rooted in the community in which they seek to serve. What that means is that when going to a new place, for the first year—at least—catechists simply listen and learn. That is very hard to do, especially for those of us who come from a Eurocentric, globalizing culture. When we are tempted, however, to enlighten those around us with the benefit of our formal education and vast experience, we need to remember how Jesus dealt with coming into a new culture: "The Word of God became man, a concrete man, in space and time and rooted in a specific culture: 'Christ by his incarnation committed himself to the particular social and cultural circumstances of the men among whom he lived' (*Ad Gentes* 10). This is the original 'inculturation' of the word of God and is the model of all evangelization by the Church" (109).

- Catechists must also draw upon the "local catechisms which respond to the demands of different cultures and which present the Gospel in relation to the hopes, questions and problems which these cultures present" (110). By "local catechisms" one assumes the GDC refers to documents such as the *National Catechetical Directory*. However, a catechist could also broaden his or her understanding of "local catechisms" to include all the practices, traditions, symbols and interactions in a culture that reflect and summarize the "hopes, questions and problems" of the people.

- Inculturation also involves "making the Catechumenate and catechetical institutes into 'centers of inculturation'" (110). This is yet another way of encouraging catechists to enter into the lives of those to be catechized. Catechetical processes are challenged to incorporate the ways of speaking and symbolizing that the people use. Catechetical processes need to incorporate the value systems of the cultures in which they exist. Obviously this must be done with some discernment. Not all cultural values are worthy ones. But catechists would do well to be careful before too quickly dismissing cultural values we find uncomfortable. The most obvious example is the practice in many cultures of beginning a meeting or event whenever everyone shows up instead of when it is "scheduled." This may seem to some of us an inefficient use of time and disrespect for those who did arrive "on time." But other cultures see scheduled times differently and find value in letting the personal interactions of the present moment take priority in their lives.

- Successful inculturation involves not only presenting the Gospel in such a way that it sounds like good news to those to whom it is proclaimed but also presenting it in such a way that those who are catechized can effectively proclaim the Gospel to those in their culture who have not yet heard the good news. In other words, the Gospel needs to not only evangelize, it must also prepare evangelists.

The integrity of the Gospel message

If the Gospel is to be effective in not only evangelizing but also in preparing evangelists, it must be presented with integrity. The most effective way to do this is for the catechist to live an integral, faithful life within the very culture he or she seeks to catechize in. Living according to the values of the culture *and* the values of the Gospel gives living witness to the possibility of following Christ within one's culture. By living out the Gospel within the culture, catechists will learn through experience how the Gospel message can be adapted and shaped—without diluting the message—to better fit the needs of the culture. "Consequently," says the GDC, "catechesis starts out with a simple proposition of the integral structure of the Christian message, and proceeds to explain it in a manner adapted to the capacity of those being catechized" (112). The catechist is, in other words, engaged in the work of "translation"—even if he or she speaks the same language as those to be catechized. The Gospel must be carefully and faithfully translated from one culture to another without either "reducing the demands" of the message or "imposing heavy burdens" which do not exist.

So what does all this mean for you as the person in charge of religious education in your parish? Let's assume you are in an older parish that was founded by people of European descent. Over the years, different ethnic groups have perhaps blended into the community, but until recently, they have also been of European descent—say, second- and third-generation Irish and Germans joining what was originally an Italian parish. Perhaps for the last 20 years or so, there has been a small minority of Spanish-speaking parishioners. Lately, however, the Spanish-speaking community has been growing. They are primarily first- and second- generation Mexicans, but there are also quite a few families that come from Guatemala and Colombia. In addition, the next-door parish has for about 10 years had a somewhat sizable Filipino population. However, an unpopular change in pastor three years ago in that parish has caused many Filipino families to start worshiping in your parish. How do you possibly meet the needs of all these different groups?

The solution is not quick or easy, but it is rich and rewarding. Follow the four concrete tasks outlined in the GDC and summarized above.

First, root yourself in the community. You may think you are rooted in the community because you have lived and worked in the same parish for 10 or 20 years. However, the community has changed. What steps have you taken to immerse yourself in the Mexican culture that has been taking root in your community? Have you also "lived" in the other Spanish-speaking cultures in your community so you know how they are alike and different from the Mexican brothers and sisters? And don't let the fact that you may not speak Spanish stand in your way. You can learn a lot about a culture simply by hanging out at their parties and liturgies. And learn what you can about the emerging Filipino culture in your parish. Filipinos have much diversity among themselves, so find out if the community in your parish has similar or differing customs and languages. Tagalog is the dominant native language, but not all Filipinos speak it. So the unifying language among all the people of those islands is English. And, since both the Mexicans and the Filipinos were colonized by the Spanish, they sometimes have similar devotional customs. If you have not already done so, spend a year—at least—going to parties, going to baptisms, hanging out after Mass, remembering birthdays and generally inserting yourself into the lives of the people in your parish.

If all this seems obvious to you because you have already immersed yourself into these ethnic communities, find those communities in your parish that you don't know so much about and become rooted in their cultures through the same kinds of practices. What saints are important to the Korean family in your parish? What are reasons for the Vietnamese to have a parade? What are the unique wedding rituals for the families from Zaire?

As you are becoming rooted in the various communities within your community, draw upon the local catechisms. What shrines do people set up in their homes? What prayers do they teach their children? What "holy days of obligation" do they have? For example, "occasional" Mexican Catholics who don't go to church even on Christmas and Easter will

show up for Our Lady of Guadalupe and Ash Wednesday. What do these kinds of "catechisms" say about their "hopes, questions and problems"?

After doing your hanging-out ministry and drawing upon the "local catechisms," you can begin to design a catechetical process that incorporates the "language, symbols, and values" of the culture. Classroom-style, text-based catechesis is not likely to be effective with any community that does not come from a Western European education model. A more *liturgical* catechesis, which reflects back the lived faith lives of the people as expressed in their worship, is much more likely to help them grow in their faith.

Then, if you can show the different communities in your parish how the cultures they come from are fertile, fruitful ground for proclaiming the Gospel, you will have begun to prepare them to be evangelizers. It is the devotion to Guadalupe as much as to Mary of the Immaculate Conception that evangelizes. It is the pious devotion to the Stations of the Cross as much as to the Advent wreath that evangelizes. And so on.

In fact, this last step permeates all the others, because, ultimately you will need to call on the members of the community to catechize the community. You cannot expect to be the lone catechist, the lone source of wisdom and faith. It is as an entire body that we carry out the mission of the Gospel. When you begin to see catechists come forth from their various cultures to catechize and evangelize those within their cultures, you will know that you have had a hand in effectively inculturating the Gospel.

For discussion

- ❏ List the four concrete tasks of inculturation. Brainstorm four strategies (one for each task) for creating a more inculturated catechetical process in your parish.
- ❏ List the different cultures that worship in your parish. What is the dominant culture? Is there a culture that is being underrepresented and underserved? How can you "hang out" with them more? Think also beyond ethnic cultures. How can you hang out with different age groups and lifestyles?

❏ What is the difference between inculturation and globalization? How are those differences reflected in your parish liturgy and catechetical processes?

The Untiring Echo: Your Catechetical Process As an E-Ticket Ride

Roman documents have an uncanny knack for saying really cool things in really dense, stuffy ways. For example: "Pedagogical instructions adequate for catechesis are those which permit the communication of the whole word of God in the concrete existence of people" (*General Directory for Catechesis* 146). In other words, the stuff we do as catechists has to connect with people's lives in such a way that they get it about who Jesus is—the whole word of God.

So what's the most effective way to communicate who Jesus is? The GDC suggests we look to the Master for "pedagogical instructions" that would be "adequate." The fundamentals of a "pedagogy of Jesus" are recorded in the Gospels, according to the GDC (140):

- *receiving* others, especially the poor and the little ones
- *proclaiming*, undiluted, the kingdom of God as good news
- *loving* in such a way that evil is defeated and life is promoted
- *inviting* others to live in faith in a way that they are impressed by the invitation
- *communicating* person to person, through word, silence, metaphor, image, example and sign

So those are our instructions: receive, proclaim, love, invite, communicate interpersonally. Do that, and people will know Jesus. Do that, and people will be catechized. It seems easy and maybe simplistic when we first look at those five actions. Don't all of us already do all those things? In fact, we don't. We do some of them, maybe all of them, sometimes. But we fail to be as disciplined as Jesus was in making his whole life a kind of walking catechesis.

I want to suggest the metaphor of theater as a lens through which to try to understand how to provide such rich experiences. However, I'm not thinking of "theater" as a dark room with a stage. I'm thinking of an experience like a ride at Disneyland. Disneyland is a magic "kingdom" where all the pedagogical actions listed in the GDC happen quite effectively. Obviously Walt Disney did not intend to catechize about Jesus, but he did intend to catechize. Disneyland is a seamless experience in which all the "actors" (not employees) stay in character and all the rides, shops, food stands, light posts, trash cans—everything—work together to provide total experience of the magic kingdom.

What would happen if we could provide a theater—an experience—of "the whole word of God" for people? What would happen if we *proclaimed* the good news that we knew of a special place, a kingdom where justice always reigned? What would happen if we could *invite* people (in an impressive way) to that place? What if, when they arrived, they discovered a place where *love* always defeats evil and where the poor are as well *received* as the wealthy? And what if while they were there, we never stepped out of character, never let our selfish nature come forth, never took off our spiritual garment and always "put on Christ"?

Well that would be just acting, wouldn't it? We don't want to playact like the "actors" at Disneyland, do we? They aren't really Mickey Mouse and Snow White, are they?

No, they aren't. But we *are* "other Christs." And we are not playacting when we are acting like Christ. The more we act like Christ, the more mature we become. Catechesis, especially a catechesis rooted in the experience of Christ in the liturgy, is a "communication of divine Revelation" (143). Catechesis is an experience of God.

It is for that reason the GDC identifies "communicating" as one of the pedagogical methods used by Jesus. Specifically, the GDC says that Jesus used "all the resources of interpersonal communication, such as word, silence, metaphor, image, example and many diverse signs" (140). These are the same tools we use in the liturgy—the place where we say that Jesus is most clearly present. It is in the drama of the liturgy where we most clearly act like Christ engaging in the "script" of interpersonal communication given to us by our tradition. Like any script, we can "act it out" well or badly. A badly performed script comes off as wooden and insincere. Good actors, however, become one with the drama they seek to enact.

If we are going to effectively enact the liturgy, the faithful must "come to it with proper dispositions, that their minds should be attuned to their voices …." The faithful must "take part, fully aware of what they are doing, actively engaged in the rite, and enriched by its effects" (*Constitution on the Sacred Liturgy* 11). In other words, we, the faithful, acting as Christ, become one with the drama of salvation. It is in that enacted moment of interpersonal communication—in the liturgy—that God most clearly engages us in a "dialogue of salvation."

That "dialogue of salvation" begins with my experience, based in my culture, and leads me— leads all of us—on a progressive journey of revelation. Several years ago, when you went to Disneyland, you got a progressive packet of tickets. You got a whole lot of A-Tickets, which were baby rides. As the tickets progressed through the alphabet—all the way up to the E-Tickets—the rides they admitted you to got more sophisticated and thrilling. If we were in the magic kingdom instead of the kingdom of God, we'd say we were on an E-Ticket ride. The Dialogue of Salvation

ride is centered on Jesus, and there is never a line to get in. There are no height or age restrictions. The whole community is on the ride together. The climax of the ride is the liturgy, where we experience sign and symbol and "where words and deeds, teaching and experience are interlinked" (143).

The role of catechesis is to "set out a synthesis to encourage a true experience of faith" (GDC 143) so the faithful understand more clearly what their role is on the Dialogue of Salvation ride. That means that effective catechesis:

- accepts the principle of the progressiveness of revelation (The Dialogue of Salvation ride has ups, downs, curves and straight-aways)
- values the community experience of faith (We're all on the ride together; no one rides alone.)
- is rooted in interpersonal relations (Not only do we all ride together, we care about our fellow riders.)
- draws its power from the reality of God's love for us (The ride never stops because God never runs out of the love that powers the ride.)

The Dialogue of Salvation ride keeps going round and round, getting better each time. Thus, "catechesis becomes an untiring echo (*Ecclesiam Suam, l.c.* 609–659)" (144) that becomes the inspiration and norm for the way we are to live. We are always in character, in a dialogue of salvation with the Father. Indeed, if we stay on the ride we will eventually abandon ourselves "completely and freely to God (*Dei Verbum* 5)" (144).

Catechists are not the only ones on the ride, of course. We aren't even in charge of the ride nor is it up to us who is allowed to ride. Everyone is invited—by the Holy Spirit—onto the ride. And everyone on the Dialogue of Salvation ride has a responsibility both to their fellow riders (the Body of Christ) and to those who don't yet know what a great ride it is. But catechists do have a particular mission to reach out to those who haven't gotten on board yet. And we have a special obligation to assist those who do climb on so they will have a better, more fulfilling, more thrilling ride.

That means our task as catechists is simple without being simplistic. Using the "pedagogy of Jesus" (receiving, proclaiming, loving, inviting, communicating), we have to find a language of invitation to those who don't know about the Dialogue of Salvation ride. We have to find "a language capable of communicating the [whole] word of God" (146) to those already on board who want a better ride. Part III, Chapter 1 of the GDC ends with another of those stuffy, but cool, statements: "Catechesis presents its service as a designated educative journey … in such a manner as to penetrate and transform the processes of intelligence, conscience, liberty and action making of existence a gift after the example of Jesus Christ" (147).

In other words, becoming one with the Body of Christ is the ride of your life.

For discussion

☐ What are the five elements of "pedagogical instruction" according to the GDC? Can you and your brainstorming team outline a pedagogical plan for the parish based on those five elements?

☐ List the resources of interpersonal communication. How effectively are these used in the liturgy? What is a specific way in which each one could be improved?

☐ Brainstorm with your team five ways in which the parish could invite more people into the dialogue of salvation.

Believing What We Pray

There is an ancient maxim that says as the church prays, so it believes. From a catechetical point of view, one might rephrase that to say the way we pray in the liturgy catechizes the parish about our faith. If that is the case, we need to take a careful look at the way in which we celebrate reconciliation.

Does our celebration of the rite of penance reflect what we believe? Or does the way in which we celebrate the rite, in reality, reflect a model of church the Second Vatican Council sought to move us beyond?

There are three ways in which most parishes celebrate this sacrament. The first is a weekly scheduled hour or two when Form I of the rite of penance is offered to individual members of the parish. Usually, a handful of parishioners come, most on a weekly basis. Anecdotal stories indicate that sins of a serious nature are seldom confessed by these weekly participants. The practice is largely devotional or reflective of an understanding that the celebration of the sacrament is always a prerequisite for sharing in communion.

The second practice is an annual gathering of all the first communion candidates for a special celebration of the sacrament, apparently intended to bring the parish into compliance with the 1973 Vatican instruction that the sacrament of penance must be administered to children before their celebration of first communion. This is usually celebrated according to Form II of the rite of penance.

The third practice is a twice-annual gathering of the parishioners in Advent and Lent to celebrate the sacrament according to Form II of the rite of penance. These celebrations are better attended in some parishes than in others, but most have plenty of seating available. In those parishes that are more successful in attracting large numbers of parishioners, the hearing of individual confessions is sometimes terminated after what the presider deems to be an appropriate amount of time, and a general absolution is administered.

What seems missing from our pastoral practice is a sense in our liturgical celebrations that the sacrament of penance flows from the continuing call to conversion that we experience in baptism. With the possible exception of the weekly devotional celebration practiced by a handful of parishioners, our parish celebrations seem to be oriented toward getting rid of the sins we've accumulated before some big event.

The *Catechism* says, "Sin is before all else an offense against God, a rupture of communion with him. At the same time it damages communion with the Church" (1440). The rite of penance says, "Those who by grave sin have withdrawn from the communion of love with God are called back in the sacrament of penance to the life they have lost" (7). The fact that most adults who celebrate this sacrament are regular communicants indicates they do not believe themselves to be in a state of serious sin. The fact that children who are preparing for first communion are, by definition, not yet in communion, makes clear they cannot be guilty of rupturing that communion.

So what is our penitential practice in our parishes intended to accomplish? It is intended to accomplish the same thing as our eucharistic practice. "Daily conversion and penance find their source and nourishment in the Eucharist .... Through the Eucharist those who live from the life of Christ are fed and strengthened" (CCC 1436).

A regular penitential practice in our parishes, then, should not have as its foundation the celebration of the sacrament of penance, nor should children be catechized to believe that it should. As important as the sacrament is, other penitential practices are more common and more central to the lives of the faithful. The *Catechism* lists these as fasting, prayer, almsgiving, concern for the poor, defense of justice, admission of faults to each other in the course of our daily relationships, perseverance, endurance, reading Scripture, praying the Lord's Prayer, acts of worship and devotion, and, of course, the celebration of the Eucharist. Yet, we tend to identify these normal and usual activities of the members of the faithful as *penitential* practices only in side comments when catechizing about the sacrament of penance. Perhaps the catechetical efforts in parishes might focus much more on developing a penitential *lifestyle* characterized by the penitential practices listed in the *Catechism* and, secondarily, provide some catechesis on less-frequent penitential *events* or moments such as the celebration of the rite of penance.

It is doubtful that such a shift in focus is possible in most parishes. Vatican, diocesan and parish policies all seem to mitigate against such a shift. But what if we could imagine how things might look in the future? What if parishes begin to re-vision the celebration of and preparation for the sacrament of penance?

In that context, parishes might look again at the practice of regularly scheduled celebrations of Form I of the rite of penance. The liturgical life of the community catechizes. Regularly scheduled celebrations of Form I say we have regular ruptures in our communion with God, when, in fact, this form of the sacrament is used mostly for devotion and seldom for actual reconciliation. The devotional needs of the small number of people who take advantage of this form of the sacrament could be adequately met by proper attention to the penitential rite of the weekday celebration of Eucharist in the parish. In those instances in which someone desires to heal an actual rupture in communion with God and the church, parish priests could be readily available just as they are when they receive a call that someone in the parish is in need of the sacrament of anointing.

A parish practice might also take another look at the requirement that children celebrate the sacrament of penance before celebrating their first communion. Besides the obvious pastoral problem of catechizing children about being reunited in a communion they have not yet celebrated, one has to seriously question the practice of making our children celebrate a sacrament that most of the adults in the community do not celebrate regularly. It is a "do as I

say, not as I do" catechesis that rings hollow and insincere.

Finally, a parish sacramental practice might look at the current use of communal celebrations in most parishes. The insistence of the celebration of the sacrament according to Form II of the rite of penance in most parishes presumes a widespread rupture in our communion with God and the church. Such is hardly ever the case. Pastorally, liturgically, ecclesiastically and catechetically, the celebration of Form III of the rite of penance seems to more clearly support a post-Vatican II model of church. Regular celebrations of Forms I and II focus us more directly on personal sin. Serious personal sin needs to be dealt with, but as a post-Vatican II church, we are on a mission to bring about the kingdom of God. Form III of the rite of penance can help us focus more directly on our corporate sin and how the social nature of our sin keeps us from fulfilling our mission. It is sometimes argued that Form III is intended to be used only in emergencies. A simple examination of the rite shows that to be a difficult position to maintain. The rite calls for a full Liturgy of the Word complete with music and singing. Several options are given for the penitential texts. The prayer of absolution itself is four paragraphs long. This is a rite that requires advance planning and rehearsal. It cannot be intended exclusively for emergencies. Most pastors and some dioceses admit as much by allowing for an on-the-spot decision to administer a general absolution when the number of participants seems too great to be accommodated in a reasonable amount of time. Lengthy celebrations may be a pastoral difficulty, but they are hardly emergencies.

These kinds of shifts in pastoral practice might be wished for by pastors and catechists for the sake of catechizing more clearly about what we believe about who God is and who we are as church. However, we live in a world of conflicting ecclesiologies. The shift in practice I'm suggesting here presumes a strong emphasis on a model of church as "the people of God" in which we are all part of a redeemed community on mission together. Current pastoral practice regarding the sacrament of penance tends more to emphasize a model of church in which each of us is continually falling from grace and in need of the intervention of the ordained priest to bring each of us, individually, back into the fold. Until we commit ourselves to a liturgical practice that more clearly reflects the Second Vatican Council's vision of the church as people of God, it is unlikely that our catechetical efforts can effectively communicate what we believe.

For discussion

❏ What forms of penance are listed in the *Catechism of the Catholic Church*? Which of these are most commonly practiced in your community? How can less common practices be encouraged?

❏ Gather your brainstorming team to read through the rite of penance. Read the introduction as well as the rite itself. What are the most appropriate uses of each of the three forms of the celebration in your community?

❏ List the various styles or models of church that are operative in your community. Which style model is dominant? Which style or model are you moving toward? How does the way in which the rite of penance is celebrated in your community catechize about a style or model of church?

Coming to Know the Mystery of Life

On the Sunday before Timothy McVeigh was executed—Trinity Sunday—this was the opening prayer we prayed at Mass:

> Father,
> you sent your Word to bring us truth
> and your Spirit to make us holy.
> Through them we come to know the mystery
>   of your life.
> Help us to worship you, One God in three Persons,
> by proclaiming and living our faith in you.

McVeigh's execution was fraught with meaning. It was the subject of endless media reports and critical analysis. It's safe to say that there isn't a Catholic in the country who was not somehow impacted by this event. And so, is it fair to ask what this prayer has to do with McVeigh's execution? Should the liturgy challenge how we think and how we live our lives in the world? And if it should, then is it fair to ask catechists to help people make that connection when they reflect on the liturgy? What can we ask the catechist to "teach" about McVeigh's execution based on the liturgy of Trinity Sunday? Did the celebration of the mystery of the Trinity challenge our thinking about this issue?

We can ask those same questions about a host of other social issues. On Trinity Sunday, the people in 28 counties in southeast Texas were flooded out of their homes. What does this prayer have to say to them?

On that same day, 32 million people in the richest nation on earth—almost the number of people that live in California—tried to survive on poverty wages.

How will this prayer help them decide between buying health insurance and shoes?

The day before, a report was released in Los Angeles that said Latinos without health insurance are routinely overcharged for medical care and prescriptions. The report noted that about 44 million Americans do not have insurance and one fourth of those are Hispanic. Does our prayer from that Sunday have any meaning for them?

What about in your own town, in your own parish, in your own family—did the opening prayer for Trinity Sunday have any meaning for you?

What does it mean?

Wouldn't a parish that believes that liturgy catechizes find in the sign of the cross a reminder of the suffering of the condemned, the flooded, the poor and the oppressed? If, in the penitential rite, we have confessed to being sinners and have heard God's reconciling word of forgiveness, shouldn't that catechize us to be forgiving toward others? Won't those of us who have publicly professed to believe in the same faith as the apostles be willing to stand up for the faith in the face of society's moral ambiguity? After we have called out over and over "Lord, hear our prayer," wouldn't the next obvious step be to prepare ourselves to allow God to use us in answering those prayers? Isn't it possible that those who take on the priesthood of Christ, offering up praise and thanksgiving, will be catechized to offer themselves as a sacrifice for the sake of the world? Isn't the catechetical effect of eating and drinking the Body and Blood of the Lord to, in Augustine's words, make us become what we eat? A parish committed to liturgical catechesis understands that we are sent forth as church to go and make the reign of God present in this time and this place. A parish that believes in effective liturgy and meaningful catechesis will find itself lobbying against the death penalty, providing relief for the homeless, working for adequate health care and generally struggling with social concerns that flow directly from our worship of the One who created the world in which we live.

That is what the opening prayer for Trinity Sunday "means." When we remind ourselves that God sent the "Word to bring us truth," we are remembering the *Logos*, the creative Word that was present "in the beginning." We are remembering the beginning when everything was in right order, a perfect harmony brought out of chaos. We are remembering the Word made flesh, sent to restore that right order we had lost. We are remembering the "truth" that we do not value what the world values. We are remembering the "truth" that God judges differently than we do.

When we remember that God sent the "Spirit to make us holy," we recall that holiness implies an obligation. We remember the Spirit that descended upon the disciples at Pentecost, propelling them to action. We remember that the Spirit inflames our spirits to do the mission Jesus left us with—the mission of restoring God's order, of establishing God's kingdom.

When we ask God to help us worship by "proclaiming and living our faith" in God, we are stating publicly, right at the beginning, that our Sunday worship only has meaning if it is reflected in the daily worship of living out our faith. We are saying that if we do not do something to point out sin and distortion of God's order that happens when we destroy life, we cannot honestly celebrate the "mystery of life" in our liturgy.

From our opening prayer to our closing song, every action and word of the liturgy should have meaning that converts our hearts and makes us holy. Every moment of the liturgy should hold a power unlike any other to restore God's order to all creation.

What do we say "Amen" to?

In fact, however, our liturgies seldom inspire us and catechize us to do ethical actions of justice. In how many places, on how many Sundays do we remember what it is we say "Amen" to in the opening prayer, in the intercessions or in the prayer after communion, for example? In how many places do our liturgical and catechetical ministries work together to provide effective reminders to us of what we promise and what we claim to stand for?

If our liturgies are not compelling us to action on behalf of the poor and the marginalized, perhaps we need to look more closely at what it is we do on Sunday. In the final analysis, the evaluation of the liturgy is not about how well the music was sung or how clearly the readings were proclaimed. It is about how many bodies were healed, how many hearts comforted, how many stomachs filled, how many spirits freed. It is about the final 15 seconds of the Mass: "Go now to love and serve the Lord." If that actually happens then the liturgy is "successful."

First steps

Celebrating liturgy that leads to justice is not an easy task. But all difficult tasks start with small steps. What small steps can you take in your parish to celebrate more effective liturgy? What steps can you take to catechize for justice? Here are two very elementary, but perhaps neglected, steps. In the liturgy, make sure no word is ever spoken frivolously or without intent. Anyone who speaks in the liturgy would want to do so with a sense of "holiness" and commitment to what the words "mean."

When catechizing, always ask the participants what they heard. Perhaps they will need to be reminded of a prayer or a song or a Scripture text. However, if they know someone will hold them accountable for remembering, they will soon begin to remember more.

Our liturgy is right worship when it has a discernable impact on our moral and ethical behavior on behalf of the poor and oppressed. Our catechetical effort is to be oriented toward making that impact a lived reality. Our ministry is ministry when it matters not only to us but to those in the world that God has sent us to serve.

For discussion

❐ Gather your brainstorming team and read the opening prayer for next Sunday. What does the prayer "mean" in the context of your community at this time in the life of the community?

❐ List the ways in which the actions of your parish liturgy connect the community to actions of justice on behalf of the poor. Brainstorm ways in which those connections could be strengthened through better liturgy or more effective catechesis.

❐ Who are the poor and the marginalized in your community? In what ways are they made welcome in the liturgy and in your catechetical processes?

Helpful Liturgical Catechesis Resources

For a regularly updated list of resources, visit http://us.geocities.com/digitalchristian/LC_resources.html.

Books

Boucher, Therese. *Evangelizing Unchurched Children: A Pocketbook for Catechists.* San Jose, Calif.: Resource Publications, Inc., 2000.

Chriszt, Dennis. *Creating an Effective Mystagogy: A Handbook for Catechumenate Leaders.* San Jose, Calif.: Resource Publications, Inc., 2001.

The Catechetical Documents: A Parish Resource. Chicago: Liturgy Training Publications, 1996. Major Roman and American catechetical documents.

Celebrating the Lectionary. San Jose, Calif.: Resource Publications, Inc., annual. Weekly guide for preachers and catechists.

Fisher, Balthasar. *Signs, Words & Gestures: Short Homilies on the Liturgy.* Translated by Matthew O'Connell. New York: Pueblo, 1981.

Guardini, Romano. *Sacred Signs.* Wilmington: Michael Glazier, 1979.

Hynes, Mary Ellen. *Companion to the Calendar.* Chicago: Liturgy Training Publications, 1993.

Jorgensen, Susan S. *Eucharist: An Eight-Session Ritual-Catechesis Experience for Adults.* San Jose, Calif.: Resource Publications, Inc., 1994.

Journals of the Catechesis of the Good Shepherd. Chicago: Liturgy Training Publications, 1998.

Lillig, Tina. *The Catechesis of the Good Shepherd in the Parish.* Chicago: Liturgy Training Publications, 1998.

Liturgical Gestures, Words, Objects: Reflections on the Liturgy in Honor of Mark Searle. Notre Dame, Ind.: Notre Dame Center for Pastoral Liturgy, 1995.

Liturgy: Central Symbols. Vol. 7, No. 1. Silver Spring, Md.: The Liturgical Conference, 1987.

The Liturgy Documents: A Parish Resource. Chicago: Liturgy Training Publications, 1997.

Liturgy: Worship That Forms Faith. Vol. 12, No. 1. Silver Spring, Md.: The Liturgical Conference, 1994. A volume devoted to worship and education.

McDonald, Mary J. *Building a Eucharistic Community: A Handbook for Liturgical Catechesis.* San Jose, Calif.: Resource Publications, Inc., 2001.

McGloin, Kevin. *What Every Catholic Needs to Know about the Mass: A Parish Guide to Liturgy.* San Jose, Calif.: Resource Publications, Inc., 2001.

McMahon Jeep, Elizabeth. *Children's Daily Prayer for the School Year.* Chicago: Liturgy Training Publications, annual.

Ostdiek, Gilbert. *Catechesis for Liturgy: A Program for Parish Involvement.* Washington, D.C.: Pastoral Press, 1986.

Philippart, David. *Savings Signs, Wondrous Words.* Chicago: Liturgy Training Publications, 1996.

Ramshaw, Gail. *Words around the Fire: Reflections on the Scriptures of the Easter Vigil.* Chicago: Liturgy Training Publications, 1990.

———. *Words around the Font: Reflections on the Scriptures of the Rite of Christian Initiation of Adults.* Chicago: Liturgy Training Publications, 1994.

———. *Words around the Table: Reflections on the Primary Actions of the Sunday Liturgy.* Chicago: Liturgy Training Publications, 1991.

Richter, Clemens. *The Meaning of the Sacramental Symbols: Answers to Today's Questions.* Translated by Linda Malloney. Collegeville, Minn.: The Liturgical Press, 1990.

Take Me Home and *Take Me Home, Too: Notes on the Church Year for Children.* Chicago: Liturgy Training Publications, 1998.

Torvend, Samuel. *Welcome Home: Scripture, Prayers, and Blessings for the Household.* 3 vols. (A B C). Minneapolis: Augsburg Fortress, 1995, 1996, 1997.

Torvend, Samuel, ed. *Passage to the Paschal Feast.* Silver Spring, Md.: The Liturgical Conference, 1992, 1993, 1994.

Wagner, Nick. *Meaningful First Communion Liturgies.* San Jose, Calif.: Resource Publications, Inc., 1998.

———. *Modern Liturgy Answers the 101 Most-Asked Questions About Liturgy.* San Jose, Calif.: Resource Publications, Inc., 1996.

Periodicals

Assembly. Bimonthly. Notre Dame Center for Pastoral Liturgy. Notre Dame, Ind.

The Catechist's Connection. Ten times yearly. Celebration Publications, Kansas City, Mo.

Catechumenate. Bimonthly. Liturgy Training Publications, Chicago.

Liturgical Catechesis. Bimonthly. Resource Publications, Inc., San Jose, Calif.

Liturgy. Quarterly journal of the Liturgical Conference. Silver Spring, Md.

Ministry & Liturgy. Ten times yearly. Resource Publications, Inc., San Jose, Calif. Includes reproducible bulletin inserts.

National Bulletin on Liturgy. Quarterly publication of the Canadian Conference of Catholic Bishops, Ottawa, Ontario, Canada.

Rite. Eight times yearly. Archdiocese of Chicago/Liturgy Training Publications. Includes reproducible bulletin inserts.